Tradition In the Making

TWINED RAG RUGS

Bobbie Irwin

Published by

krause publications

700 E. State St.
Iola, WI 54990-0001
Telephone 715-445-2214
www.krause.com

Please call or write for our free catalog. Our toll-free number to place an order or obtain a free catalog is 800-258-0929 or please use our regular business telephone 715-445-2214 for editorial comment and further information.

Library of Congress Catalog Number: 00-101576

ISBN: 0-87341-898-0

Printed in the United States of America

Dedication

In Memory of Lillie Sherwood
1900-1993

Lillie Sherwood

Acknowledgments

As my car bumped along a dirt road, headed toward an Idaho ranch I'd never visited before, I hoped that no one would be home. Fortunately, someone was. Little did I expect that my "chance" meeting with 80-year-old Lillie Sherwood during the 1980 census would redirect my life and involve me in a fascinating research project and a crusade to revive an almost-forgotten folk art. This book is one result.

I didn't choose to study twined rag rugs, I was chosen. That must be why I took the job as a census-taker (something I'd normally avoid); otherwise, I never would have met Lillie. I wasn't interested in rag rugs, and I certainly never intended to specialize in them. That changed when I stepped inside Lillie's home and discovered the most beautiful and unusual rag rugs I'd ever seen. I was delighted to learn she had made them; she was delighted that I was interested, and she invited me to watch as she deftly twisted strips of fabric around strands suspended on a simple frame.

Lillie didn't have a name for her method, but because I was a weaver, I recognized it as *twining*. Eventually, when I realized how uncommon and unusual these rugs really were, I returned and learned everything I could about rag twining.

It must have been my destiny to learn from the best. Few others have ever approached Lillie's level of skill, masterful use of color, and inventive patterning. If I'd seen someone else's twined rag rugs first, I might not have paid any attention to them. Lillie Sherwood, my mentor, friend, and surrogate grandmother, passed on to me her equipment as well as her knowledge, and it has been a privilege to make some of my rugs on her frame.

In the years since I first saw Lillie Sherwood's twined rugs, I have located many others. I am grateful to all the generous people who have shared their information, experience, memories, photographs, and rugs with me. I also appreciate the assistance of museum personnel, authors, and textile experts who have

helped make this book possible.

Special thanks go to Linda Heinrich, for her extensive work on my behalf, documenting rugs in the Royal British Columbia Museum; and to John Veillette, Anthropology Collections Manager at the same facility, for his patient assistance and insight. I thank Janet Meany and Paula Pfaff, rag rug experts who have provided many valuable contacts and resources; and Silvia Falett, for helping trace rug traditions on two continents and reintroducing the craft in Europe.

I'm grateful to my husband, Reed Irwin, for his support, along with photography and technical assistance (including writing instructions for equipment he constructed), and for helping to keep me on track.

For those who here discover twined rag rugs for the first time, and to all who have asked for a book, I hope this material will answer your questions and will inspire your continued interest, so that this worthwhile craft will bring enjoyment to future generations.

Contents

Chapter 1: An Introduction to Twining 6
What Is Twining? 7
What Is a Twined Rag Rug? 9
Rag Twining Terminology 9
How Do I Recognize a Twined Rug? 10

Chapter 2: Equipment & Materials 11
Frame Types 11
Pegged Frames 11
Unpegged Frames 12
Frames With Rollers 12
Curved Frames 14
Conventional Looms for Twining 14
Twining Without a Frame 15
Selvedge Guides 16
Building Small Frames for Samplers 16
Building Full-Sized Frames 17
Pegged and Plain Frames 17
Adjustable Unpegged Frames 17
Frame with Suspended Wires 18
Salish Loom 20
Other Equipment 22
Warp Materials & Preparation 24
Fabric Vs. String Warp 24
Warp Width 25
Warp Joins 25
How Much Warp Do I Need? 26
Weft Materials & Preparation 27
Choice of Fabric 27
Weft Width 27
How Much Weft Do I Need? 28
Fabric Patterns & Colors 28
Sources for Fabrics 30
Weft Joins 31

Chapter 3: Learning to Twine 33
Warping 33
Method #1: Continuous Warp 33
Method #2: Warp Loops 34
Method #3: Individual Warps 35
Warp Tension 36
An Odd or Even Number of Warps? 36

When Do I Have Enough Warps? 37
General Twining Instructions 37
How Long Does It Take? 37
Weft Length & Joins 37
Twining in Various Directions 38
Working From Both Ends 38
Finishing a Rug 39
Twining Large Rugs 40
Learning by Sampling 40
Regular Twining 41
Sampler #1: Countered Twining, Solid Stripes, and Edge-Turn Variations 44
Same-Pitch Twining 48
Sampler #2: Same-Pitch Twining 49
Three-Weft Twining 52
Sampler #3: Three-Weft Countered Twining 53
Sampler #4: False Tapestry 56
Tapestry 58
Sampler #5: Countered Tapestry Twining 59
Taaniko 63
Sampler #6: Countered Taaniko 64
Salish-Style Twining 67
Sampler #7: Salish-Style Twining 68
Circular Twining 72
Sampler #8: Circular Twining 73
Oval Twining 75
Sampler #9: Oval Twining 76
Caring for Twined Rag Rugs 79

Chapter 4:
Projects 80

Turquoise Nuggets 81
Barefoot Delight 84
Remembering Lillie 86
Just Jeans 88
Twined and Intertwined 90
Canyon Country 94
Spirit of the Northwest 98
North Star 102
Celebration 106
Sunset 109
Designing Your Own Rugs 112

Chapter 5:
A Celebration of Rug Twiners 113

Introduction 113
Lillie Sherwood 118
Leona Christensen Lambert 120
Grace Kenfield 120
Virginia Verdier 122
Grace Durfee 122
Nathan Jones 124
Mary Peters 124
Fred Gossell 126
Silvia Falett 127
Rag Twining Today 127

About the Author 128

Chapter 1

An Introduction to Twining

More than a century ago, creative people adapted an ancient textile art, *twining*, to a new purpose, by twisting strips of fabric around perpendicular strands to make twined rag rugs. At virtually no cost, twining requires only homemade equipment, common household tools, and scrap fabric. It produces a heavy, sturdy rug that someone of any age can make, regardless of education, experience, or income. Although it takes some time to complete a rug, rag twining is a good spare-time project that doesn't require extended work periods.

A twined rag rug meets all the characteristics of a good rug:

A good rug should be durable. It is meant to be walked on and should be designed for hard use. With proper care, a three-layered twined rag rug will last for decades, longer than many other rag rugs.

A good rug should be heavy and should stay put without curling at the corners. Heavier than most loom-woven rag rugs, a

Hit-and-miss rug by Lillie Sherwood, Clayton, Idaho, 1970s.

twined rug's weight and nubby texture help keep it in place. Properly designed, it lies absolutely flat — an important safety feature.

A good rug is attractive. Rugs are utilitarian, yet I think it's important that something we spend a lot of time to create, and something we use every day, should also be beautiful. Even simple twined rag rugs have a special appeal, and twining provides the potential for some exciting and intricate patterns rarely found in other rag rugs.

WHAT IS TWINING?

Twining is similar to weaving and shares much of the same terminology. Twined and woven items have lengthwise strands called *warps*, which form the framework, and crosswise strands called *wefts*, which usually travel back and forth and connect the warps to form a textile. (*The warp* may mean a single warp strand or all of the warps together. *Warping* means aligning the warps, usually by placing them under tension on a frame or loom.) Warps and wefts are usually parallel to themselves and perpendicular to each other, except in basketry where the warps may radiate from a central point and the wefts spiral out from the center (even in baskets, the warps are normally perpendicular to the wefts). In all the diagrams, the warps are shown as the vertical strands and the wefts as the horizontal strands.

Just as *twine* is a twisted cord, twining involves twisting. If warps twist to enclose wefts, the technique is called *warp twining*. When wefts twist around each other to enclose the warps, the structure is *weft twining*. Weft twining, the most common type, is used to make twined rag rugs. Unlike most forms of weaving, weft twining requires at least two wefts that travel in the same direction at the same time and cross each other to form a row.

Decorative rag twining by Wendy E. Bateman, Haliburton, Ontario. The piece incorporates tapestry with taaniko, and was left on the frame for permanent display. Courtesy Wendy E. Bateman.

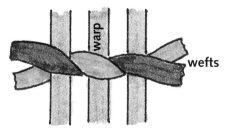

Weft twining

Twined wefts "do all the work" while the warp usually stays in one place. Where they cross the warps, the wefts usually completely enclose and hide them. *Compact twining* results when rows are closely packed; if the twined rows are spaced, the warp shows between the rows (*spaced twining*). Twined rag rugs are constructed with compact twining to make a dense, durable carpet.

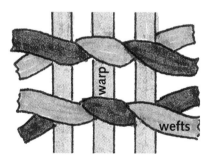

Compact twining

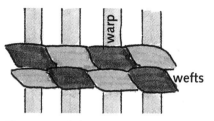

Spaced twining

Weft twining creates distinctive textures and patterns that vary with the methods used. A weft passes over one or more warps before crossing another weft in the space between warps. This creates a *weft segment* (the portion of weft that appears on the surface) with a distinctive slant.

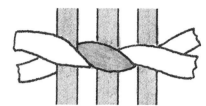

The turquoise section is one weft segment.

Left-pitch weft segments slant up to the left; *right-pitch* weft segments slant up to the right.

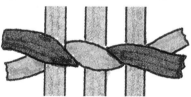

Left-pitch twining. Where the turquoise weft crosses the warp, it slants up to the left.

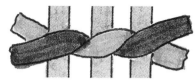

Right-pitch twining. Where the turquoise weft crosses the warp, it slants up to the right.

If the pitch remains the same in successive rows (*same-pitch twining*), the texture appears uniform. If the pitch changes from one row to the next, the variation (*countered twining*) produces a chevron-like texture.

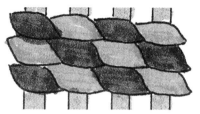

Same-pitch twining

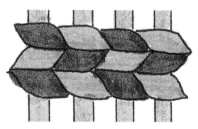

Countered twining

Of the dozens of variations of weft twining, very few were ever used for rag rugs. Many twining methods that are practical with relatively fine yarn or basketry materials do not adapt well to rag twining because of the bulk and flexibility of the fabric or the intended use of the finished item. Few rugmakers have known more than one or two twining methods. Undoubtedly there are other variations besides those mentioned here that you could adapt to make interesting and practical rugs.

Twining is extremely ancient, older than ordinary weaving and dating back more than 25,000 years. The oldest fabrics ever discovered were twined, and even older evidence is found as impressions of twined objects in clay and pottery. Twining seems to have been a universal craft with many independent origins, a natural way for people to assemble flexible materials.

In certain cultures, twining became an art form. The Maori of New Zealand and the people of the Pacific Northwest and Africa are renowned for their elaborate twining. In most industrialized nations, twining has virtually disappeared except in basketry, where it still flourishes. In America, few people are familiar with twining unless they make baskets (or twined rag rugs!).

WHAT IS A TWINED RAG RUG?

A twined rag rug is one in which two (rarely more) fabric-strip wefts twist around each other to enclose warps of string, heavy cord, yarn, or fabric. Warps are hidden except at the top and bottom of a rug. Most twined rag rugs have four finished edges and have been made on simple frames with warps under tension. A few rugs have been made on horizontal looms, on tapestry looms, on free-hanging or weighted warps, on hoops, or without any support for the warps. While most twined rag rugs are rectangular, some are curved.

Rag twining is a versatile technique not restricted to rugs, although most rag-twined items are floor coverings. People have also twined fabric for upholstery, furniture pads, bed covers, saddle girths, carrying straps, wall hangings, frames, baskets, bags, and fencing.

Bedspread by Nathan Jones, Maeser, Utah. Courtesy Nathan Jones.

Twined rag chair cover by Avis Larson, Cloquet, Minnesota. Courtesy Avis Larson.

RAG TWINING TERMINOLOGY

It's ironic that almost nobody who ever made twined rag rugs called the technique *twining* or the rugs *twined*. Few references mention the correct terms, although some call the method *twined weaving* or *twined plaiting*, and only rugmakers familiar with twining from other sources have called their rugs *twined*.

Because the texture of twining resembles braiding, rag twining is often called *frame braiding, braid weaving,* or *twined plaiting*. One reference used the term *herringbone weave* because of a superficial resemblance to a quite different woven fabric. Authors have called twining *cross weaving, pairing, paring, wattling,* and *Indian tie weaving*. Many rugmakers have just called the process weaving; some have had no name at all for the technique.

I use informal names for twining variations, with diagrams to clarify the meanings. My term *regular twining* describes the most common technique used for rag rugs: using two wefts that cross with a half twist to enclose single warps, and that travel from side to side in countered twining. A regular turn is the normal way two wefts travel around a selvedge. This doesn't mean that other methods are irregular! In the book I talk about several techniques, including *taaniko*, the Maori method for twining intricate patterns.

Throughout the book, when I refer to *hit and miss*, I mean a random color pattern, or a rug with a random pattern.

In many cases, I recommend *sampling*, which means testing a fabric strip for proper width by twining a row or two, or twining a small item to practice a technique.

Traditionally, rag rugs were truly made with *rags* — scraps of fabric salvaged from worn-out clothing. In this book, rag simply means fabric, whether old or new. A rag rug is made primarily from cloth.

You will also see the word *selvedge* used frequently. The selvedge is simply the side of a textile or rug, or the warp at the side; a finished edge formed when wefts turn around the edge warp.

Standard loom refers to conventional weaving equipment — usually with heddles, which raise or lower warp threads. A *frame* is a simpler device that usually lacks ways to adjust tension, move warp strands up and down, or advance a warp. Some tapestry looms and Salish looms (see page 20) can tension and advance a warp. See Chapter 2 for detailed information and illustrations of twining equipment.

I did not know [the rugs] were called "twined." I'm glad to hear a name for them other than "the rugs I make."

Ramona Brubaker,
St. George, Utah

HOW DO I RECOGNIZE A TWINED RUG?

It's easy to confuse the dozens of kinds of rag rugs, some of which are made on frames like twined rugs. Twined rag rugs tend to be heavier, thicker, and denser than many other rag rugs, with a nubby texture. A twined rug has three layers. The warp, the center layer, is hidden and sandwiched between two layers of weft.

Braided, false-braided, knitted, crocheted, and nålbinded ("toothbrush") rugs all lack the perpendicular core (warp) of a twined rug. A rug made of narrow rows sewn together is probably not twined. Unlike twined rugs, in most woven rugs the warp shows on the surface and wefts don't normally cross at regular intervals. Most woven rugs have only one weft per row. Woven Shaker rugs have twisted wefts, but the wefts don't enclose the warps. In a few woven rugs, a weft wraps around the warp, but there is only one weft per row.

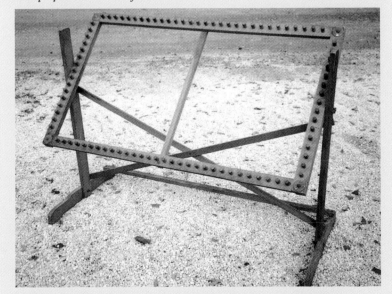

Chapter 2

Equipment & Materials

Rag twining requires only simple, homemade equipment and inexpensive materials. Your choice of frame will depend on equipment you may already have, your tools and carpentry skills, your storage space, the size rugs you want to make, and the twining techniques you prefer. Your physical limitations may also dictate the equipment that is most comfortable.

There are many frame variations. I'll describe the more common types and give you instructions for making some of them. Feel free to improvise!

FRAME TYPES

Pegged Frames

Most twined rag rugs have been made on rectangular frames with outside dimensions slightly larger than the rugs. Most of these frames support the warp with nails or dowels across the top and bottom, usually an inch apart and protruding at least an inch, for a spacing of two warps per inch. A few frames space the warp with notches, cuphooks, rug canvas, or safety pins in fabric strips fastened to the crossbars. For convenience, I'll call all these variations *pegged* frames.

The chief advantage of pegged frames is ease of construction and warping. Most rugs made on pegged frames have four finished edges, since you can twine right up to the pegs. Most pegged frames limit the size of a rug and prevent tension adjustments as you work.

Since pegged frames predetermine warp spacing, it's easy to calculate warp length ahead of time. It's important to cut fabric strips so that they will

*I*n the 1940s, Sears & Roebuck marketed (for $2.98!) the Hearthside Adjustable Rug Frame, which may have been designed for twining. This pegged frame, with a stand to support it at a comfortable working angle, had heavy dowels evenly spaced on all four sides.

Hearthside Adjustable Rug Frame. Courtesy Penny Myers, Akron, Ohio.

give the proper spacing when twined, or to adjust the tightness of the twining to keep the warps aligned. Since I like to let fabrics determine their own spacing, I rarely use a pegged frame. Because *taaniko* twining (see page 63) tends to pull wefts especially tight, I do not recommend pegged frames for taaniko or for rugs with stretchy weft fabric, unless you are very careful not to twine too tightly.

Unpegged Frames

An unpegged frame is the simplest to construct and lets the fabric determine its own spacing, making it a good choice for taaniko and stretchy wefts. Warping and twining are a little more difficult than on a pegged frame. The inside width and length of a plain frame are the maximum practical dimensions for a rug. You can wrap the warp around the frame and leave it as fringe, or tuck the ends back into the rug.

Suspending crosswise rods or wires from a frame lets you make rugs shorter than the frame. The wires hold the warp while you're working and you pull them out when the rug is done. Thick rods leave loops of warp at the top and bottom of a rug, which you should fill with fringe or additional rows of twining after you remove a rug from the frame (a tricky proposition!). Music (piano) wire, supported at regular intervals, leaves insignificant loops. Available in three-foot lengths at hobby stores that sell model supplies, music wire is much stiffer than other wire of com-

parable diameter, so it is less likely to bend.

Overlap sections of wire for rugs wider than three feet. Most frames with wires let you adjust warp tension as you work, and you can make rugs of different sizes and warp spacings on the same frame.

Frames With Rollers

A Salish-style loom, with horizontal dowels mounted between uprights, is a practical design that saves space and lets

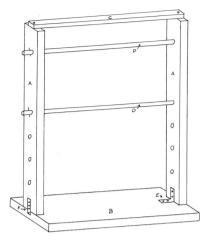

you make long rugs. You can move the warp around the

Lillie Sherwood's unpegged rug frame.

There are many elaborate examples of twining from the Pacific Northwest. Perhaps the oldest twined rag rugs still in existence are Salish (pronounced "say-lish") Indian rugs in the Smithsonian Institution. Salish people, of many different cultures and speaking different dialects, are related by language. Collected in the Puget Sound area by James G. Swan in 1875, several of these rugs show signs of wear and most were probably created before 1870.

Although Salish rugmakers may have seen rag rugs in settlers' homes, the patterning and same-pitch twining in Salish rugs reflect their own twining traditions and are quite different from rugs with a European influence. Salish weavers started using strips of commercial fabric as a decorative accent in their textiles as soon as trade cloth became available, and they were probably among the first people to twine rag rugs, starting sometime in the late 1850s. They made most of their rugs on upright frames with rollers. In 1887, Myron Eels, a missionary and amateur anthropologist, described and sketched Salish rugs from the Puget Sound area. His is the oldest reference to twined rag rugs I have found.

Detail of Salish rug collected by James G. Swan in 1875. Catalogue No. 23428, Department of Anthropology, Smithsonian Institution. Photo by Bobbie Irwin.

White missionaries and other settlers of British Columbia discouraged "primitive" Salish crafts and introduced "civilized" crafts such as knitting and embroidery. However, rag rugs were a useful household accessory, so Salish people were able to continue their twining traditions by making rag rugs to sell and trade, at least into the 1920s.

While living in Vancouver, British Columbia, in the 1930s, Mary McNeill Sieburth became concerned about the decline of native crafts and acquired a large collection, including a number of Salish twined rag rugs bequeathed to the Royal British Columbia Museum in 1985.

Salish rug from the Mary McNeill Sieburth Collection. Catalogue # 18703, Royal British Columbia Museum.

dowels as you work, keeping the working area at a convenient height. Hannah Barcus, a twiner from Minnesota, uses a similar upright frame. She wraps a circular warp around large rollers and cuts the finished rug off the frame.

Reverse warping (see Chapter 3) around a single wire lets you make a rug twice as long as the distance between the dowels, with four finished edges. There's no need to flip the frame over to work from each end, as you do with a pegged or plain frame. Warping around two suspended wires makes rugs of varying lengths.

Curved Frames

Some people twine rugs on hoops such as wagon wheels and bicycle wheel rims. Radial warps cross in the center and are fastened to the rim to hold them taut; twining spirals out from the center. Large embroidery hoops and circular knitting frames might be adapted to make small twined rugs. You can also tack radiating warps to rectangular frames.

Conventional Looms for Twining

You can adapt upright tapestry looms for twining. They function much like Salish looms, and some let you move and store extra warp on rollers.

If you have a standard floor or table loom, you may find it comfortable for twining. Because twining is a hand-manipulated technique, a conventional loom doesn't speed the process, and most people who have made twined rugs have not had access to looms.

Heddles and treadles aren't needed. Remove the heddle frames ("harnesses") if possible, or move all the heddles out of the way or distribute them evenly between warp strands. The beater is optional for packing weft rows. A coarse reed (4, 5, or 6 dents per inch) will help keep warps aligned if you're using yarn, string or nonraveling fabric warp that isn't too bulky. On a loom, the twining motion is away from you, like working from the bottom of a frame upwards, so you may need to alter the directions and illustrations in this book.

A standard loom lets you advance the warp and make long rugs (provided storage space on your cloth beam is adequate) as wide as the normal weaving width of the loom. Warp with a cross, allowing extra, as for other weaving. Leave warp as fringe, or needleweave warps in later. Without a reed, using a continuous or looped warp between wires, you can work from both ends of some looms to make a rug with four finished edges.

Turquoise Nuggets (see Chapter 4, Projects) being twined on a floor loom; the heddles have been removed.

Twined rag rug from the Mary McNeill Sieburth Collection. Catalogue #18710, Royal British Columbia Museum.

Nuu-chah-nulth twined rag rug, possibly made in the late 1950s. Catalogue #16335, Royal British Columbia Museum.

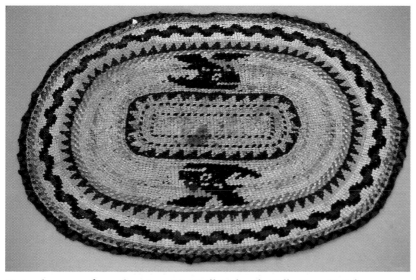

Twined rag rug from the Mary McNeill Sieburth Collection. Catalogue #18708, Royal British Columbia Museum.

Twining Without a Frame

Warps don't have to be under tension while you work. Some old rugs were twined on loose warps hung from a bar suspended in a doorway. Curved rugs from the Pacific Northwest were probably made basketry-fashion, without a frame.

In addition to rugs twined on Salish looms, the Royal British Columbia Museum preserves newer rugs attributed to Nuu-chah-nulth (pronounced "new-cha-noolth") twiners of western Vancouver Island, a geographically isolated region where rug twining apparently persisted into the mid-1900s. The Nuu-chah-nulth ("Nootka") people are one of many Pacific Northwest cultures with twining traditions.

Most of these rugs are oval, elaborately patterned with geometric and realistic designs derived from basketry, including birds, whales, canoes, and mythical creatures. Acquired by the museum between 1945 and 1985, some were collected by Mary Sieburth and some came from other sources. It's unknown when and where they were created, but one may have been made as late as the 1950s. Although I've seen a few round and oval rugs elsewhere, I know of no other rugs in the world that exhibit such mastery of pattern and technique.

SELVEDGE GUIDES

It's difficult to maintain straight selvedges, especially when making long rugs, when introducing complicated patterning, when twining with stretchy materials or wefts of varying elasticity, or when combining taaniko and regular twining. To combat this problem, numerous twiners add selvedge guides to the sides of pegged and plain frames. Pegs are the simplest guides, spaced 1″ to 4″ apart. Place the edge warps outside the pegs, hook weft rows onto the side pegs, or both. Some twiners lace the selvedges of a rug to the sides of the frame at regular intervals, or twine around the sides of a frame for a rug with fringed sides.

Side pegs are not adequate selvedge guides when twining tightly with stretchy fabrics, especially for taaniko, which tends to pull the wefts very tight. For stiffer support, use music wire placed through screw eyes on the side boards. Bend wires at the top to stay in place and provide grips for removal. Twine wefts around the wire and selvedge warps together (but don't wrap a weft around the shank of a screw eye).

As long as a rug stays flat while you are working, wires do a good job of keeping the sides straight. If the work is distorted on the frame because of unbalanced weft widths, complex patterning, uneven twining tension, or differences in weft elasticity, there will be some selvedge distortion no matter what selvedge guide you've used.

BUILDING SMALL FRAMES FOR SAMPLERS

Most of the sampler projects in Chapter 3 use small frames made from inexpensive stretcher bars (canvas stretchers), available from art and hobby suppliers. Purchase six 11″ sections so you can assemble several different types of frames.

On the top section of a pegged frame, nail eight 1″ brads (small finishing nails) about 3/8″ up from the bottom (inside) edge and starting 1/4″ from the left inside corner. If using wood harder than the pine typically used for canvas stretchers, drill starter holes for the nails so the wood won't split. Space the brads 1″ apart, extending about 5/8″. Hammer eight brads in the bottom section, starting 3/4″ from the left inside corner. This staggers the nails at the top and bottom for even warp alignment.

Don't fasten the frames together permanently; you'll replace the pegged sections with plain stretcher bars to experiment with different warping methods. For two of the samplers in Chapter 3, you will also need two pieces of stiff wire a little wider than the inside of the frame. Most stretcher bars have angled, notched ends that fit together to form a frame with mitered corners.

For Sampler #7 (page 68), you will need a Salish-style frame made from two 8″ pieces of 1″ x 2″ lumber and two 5/8″ dowels, each 9″ long. Sand all parts well. With the sides clamped together, drill perpendicular holes centered 1-1/8″ from each end, to hold the dowels snugly. You'll also need a piece of stiff wire just narrower than the inside of the frame. See detailed construction instructions for a full-size Salish-style frame on page 20.

This pegged frame shows eight brads inserted in the top and bottom sections.

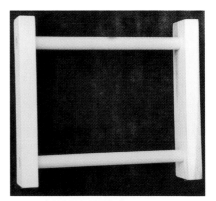

Salish sampler frame.

BUILDING FULL-SIZED FRAMES

Pegged & Plain Frames

Stretcher bars also work for large frames, since they are available in lengths of up to 6′ or 8′. An assortment of sizes will let you make frames of different dimensions. Fasten the stretcher bars together securely while in use (most stores supply corner wedges with the stretchers). For any pegged frame, peg spacing is your choice; 1″ spacing is traditional. Stagger the pegs so those at the bottom are halfway between those at the top.

For a large frame, 1″ x 2″ lumber is strong enough and less expensive than canvas stretchers. Holes in the sides let you adjust pegged crossbars to different positions, holding them in place with bolts and wingnuts. The distance between the top and bottom pegs is the maximum length of a rug. The length of the crossbars determines the maximum width, which can exceed the distance between the sides of the frame. Nails with heads keep the warp from slipping off; headless nails or dowels make it easier to remove a rug. Instructions for the frame with suspended wires (below) can be adapted for pegged or plain frames as well, without using eyebolts and wires.

You can use a sturdy, flat picture frame for twining. Window frames, curtain stretchers, quilting frames, and rug-hooking frames may work. Although there is not a lot of stress on a frame during twining, it needs to withstand a little tension. The larger the frame, the more support it needs.

I've seen an unpegged frame constructed from PVC pipe, using standard pipe fittings in the corners. If the crossbars are not glued in place, you can remove a rug by disassembling the corners and slipping the rug off the pipe.

Adjustable Unpegged Frames

The two self-supporting frames described below accommodate rugs of many different sizes, including all the projects in this book. Both come apart for storage (mark all parts for reassembly). When buying lumber, choose straight boards with as few knots as possible. The standard lumber sizes given are larger than actual dimensions (for example, a 2″ x 4″ is actually 1-1/2″ x 3-1/2″ and a 1″ x 2″ is actually 3/4″ x 1-1/2″).

An adjustable pegged frame used by Virginia Verdier, Sidney, Ohio. Courtesy Virginia Verdier.

All holes must be perpendicular (I strongly advise using a drill press), boards must be cut straight across, and each wood piece must be well-sanded. A wood finish is optional but if you choose to apply a finish, do it before assembly and don't apply varnish inside the drill holes. Refer to the table below for the materials needed.

Tools needed include a wood saw, drill press, electric hand drill, assorted drill bits, screwdriver, carpenter square, tape measure, sandpaper, clamps, vise, pliers, and pencil. You may adapt these instructions for a larger or smaller frame.

Frame With Suspended Wires

This frame accommodates rugs up to 30" x 54" and mounts sideways on the same supports for wide rugs. It rotates for twining from both ends (always work on the same side of a rug). The wires and optional selvedge guides adjust for many different sizes of rug.

To Assemble the Frame and Supports:

Mark a center line (lengthwise) on the narrow side of two 60" and two 36" 1" x 2"s. On the center line of each piece, mark the midpoint and drill-hole locations at 6" intervals in both directions from the midpoint (do not mark the ends). Drill a 1/4" diameter hole through each board at each mark.

Using the four sections you've drilled, construct a frame 60" x 39". With the wide sides up on a flat surface, butt the 39" sections inside the 60" sides and mark the four boards for assembly. Place the metal corner braces in position and mark the drill-hole locations for the corner braces, adjusting the braces so no hole overlaps a joint. Drill 3/16" holes at each location and fasten a brace on the front and back sides of the frame at each corner, using the #10 x 1-1/4" machine screws and nuts.

For the two support uprights, use the two 37" sections of 1" x 2". At one end of each piece, draw a 7" line down the center of the wide side. Mark and drill 1/4" holes 1" and 7" from the end, using the drawn line to center the holes. At the opposite end of each board, mark and drill hole locations (offset) for wood screws, to at-

tach the 24" 2" x 4" support bases. Center each base perpendicular to the upright, wide sides together to form a T. Mark and drill pilot holes, smaller than the screws, and attach the bases.

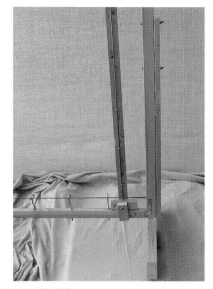

Detail of frame with suspended wires, showing supports.

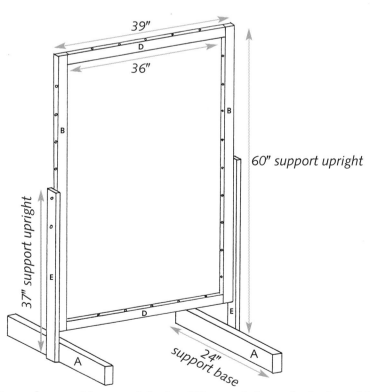

Frame for use with suspended wires. Wires, eyebolts, and selvedge guides not shown. Letters refer to materials list. Illustration by Reed Irwin.

Attach the supports to the frame at the top of the upright with two 1/4″ stove bolts on each side, with the top bolts through the middle holes in the frame, and the support base 2″ x 4″s toward the inside. To rotate the frame during twining, temporarily loosen the top bolts and remove the lower bolts.

Insert eyebolts to extend to the inside of the frame through the holes at the top and bottom. The eyebolts support the heavier wires which hold the warp. The bottom eyebolts need nuts both inside and outside the frame to keep them extended during warping. Use as many eyebolts as needed for your project to support the 3mm wires just beyond the width of the rug. Overlap wires for wide rugs.

Open 12 of the eyebolts slightly so the wire will slide easily into them. Use unopened eyebolts to support the wires at the center and sides of the warp, with opened bolts in between, allowing adjustment of the warp on the wire. Adjust nuts to keep wires parallel to the ends of the frame. For short rugs, use threaded rod and coupling nuts to lengthen the eyebolts as needed.

Selvedge Guides:
Construct two long selvedge guides from the two remaining 60″ pieces of 1″ x 2″.

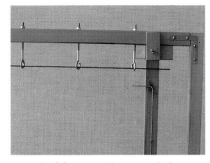

Detail of frame with suspended wires, showing eyebolts and selvedge guide.

For clamps, cut eight 4″ and eight 3″ pieces from the leftover 1″ x 2″.

Materials for Frame With Suspended Wires

	Quantity	Size	Type/Description	Comments & Diagram Reference
Wood	1	2″ x 4″ x 4′	pine or fir	2 pieces 24″ each (support bases, A)
(keep all	4	1″ x 2″ x 8′	pine or fir	4 pieces 60″ each
cut-off pieces)				(sides, B, & long selvedge guides, C)
				(use 2 of the remaining 36″ pieces for tops & base, D)
	2	1″ x 2″ x 8′	pine or fir	2 pieces 37″ each (support uprights, E) plus 2 pieces 39″ each (short selvedge guides, F)
Hardware				
	18	1/4″ x 5″	eyebolts	with matching nuts
	18	1/4″ x 8″	threaded rod	same thread as eyebolts
	18	1/4″	rod coupling nuts	same thread as eyebolts
	4	1/4″ x 2-3/4″	stove or machine bolts	same thread as eyebolts
	13	1/4″	nuts	same thread as eyebolts
	8	#10 x 2-1/2″	machine screws	with matching wingnuts
	16	#10 x 1-1/4″	machine screws	with matching nuts
	4	#8 x 1-1/2″	wood screws	
	8	3″	flat corner braces	
	36	1″	screw eyes	
	4	3mm x 36″	music wire	to hold warp
	6	2mm x 36″	music wire	for selvedge guides

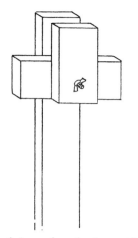

Detail of clamp for selvedge guide. The letter B refers to materials list. Illustration by Reed Irwin.

On the wide side of each 60" selvedge guide, mark a perpendicular line 1-1/2" from both ends. Glue a 4" block inside of and flush with one of the lines, perpendicular to the guide. After the glue dries, place the guide against the frame with the block tight against the inside edge and parallel to the bottom of the frame. The mark at the other end of the guide should be flush with the inside of the opposite end of the frame (adjust as needed). Glue another 4" block to this end. Drill perpendicular 3/16" holes through each block and guide.

On one end of each selvedge guide, place a 3" block centered on the 4" block, parallel with the guide, flush with the inner edge and extending beyond the other edge of the longer block. Mark the hole location and drill a 3/16" hole. Attach the 3" block on top of the 4" block with a #10 x 2-1/2" machine screw and wingnut. Repeat for each end of each guide.

On the face (wide side) of each selvedge guide, mark the

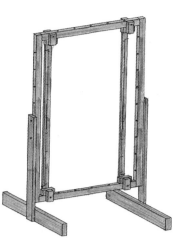

Frame with selvedge guides and selvedge wires in place. The top and bottom wires (which support the warp) and the eyebolts that hold the wires are not shown. Illustration by Reed Irwin.

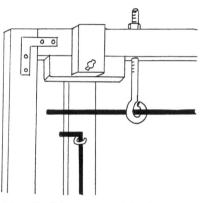

Detail of the corner of the frame, showing the top of one selvedge guide, selvedge wire, and suspended wire to hold the warp.

center 27" from one 4" block, then mark every 6" in both directions. Drill 3/32"-diameter holes about 1/2" deep at each mark and attach screw eyes, leaving the center of each eye about 3/8" above the surface and open to the length of the guide. At each end of a guide, open the last two eyes slightly toward the outsides, wide enough to insert the finer selvedge wire.

Using the 39" pieces of 1" x 2" and the same steps, con-

struct shorter selvedge guides for use when the frame is turned sideways.

Make a sharp bend about 1-1/2" from the end of each 2mm wire. Since this wire is very stiff, clamp it in a vise before you try to bend it. Insert the wire through the screw eyes with the bend resting on the top screw eye. Overlap wires as needed for long rugs; you may want to install the second wire after you rotate the frame, so its bent end is up. To adjust guides for twining, loosen the wingnuts and slide the guides sideways, keeping them parallel to the sides of the frame. The distance between the wires should be the desired width of the rug.

Salish Loom

This compact frame is for rugs up to 3' wide and 6' long. Mark a lengthwise line down the center of the wide side of each of the 48" pieces. These are the side pieces. With a drill press, drill perpendicular holes centered 7-1/2", 13-1/2", 19-1/2", 25-1/2", and 41-1/4" from the bottom of each piece (the holes must be slightly larger than the dowels, so the dowels will move freely).

Position the sides vertically on the ends of the base, centered and perpendicular. If the base is warped, place the concave side down. Position the corner braces on the insides at the base, centered. Mark screw holes on each board, drill pilot holes smaller than the screws (hole depth about equal to screw length), and screw the corner braces in place. Center the mending plates vertically across the outside contact between the sides and base. The screw holes should not overlap the joints or other screws. Mark and drill pilot holes and attach the plates.

Center the 40" wooden brace across the top, ends flush with the outside of the side pieces. Mark the location of screw holes 3/4" in from each end, centered. Drill pilot holes and screw the brace onto the sides with the 1-1/2" screws.

Insert a dowel through the top holes on the sides, extending equal amounts on each side. The rod should rotate easily in the holes. Mark each end about 1/4" beyond the sides; drill a hole (centered) with a 1/8" bit through the rod at each mark. Repeat with the other rod. When the frame is in use, insert a finishing nail through each hole, extending equally on each side of the rod, and secure with a rubber band. Remove nails temporarily to reposition the rods.

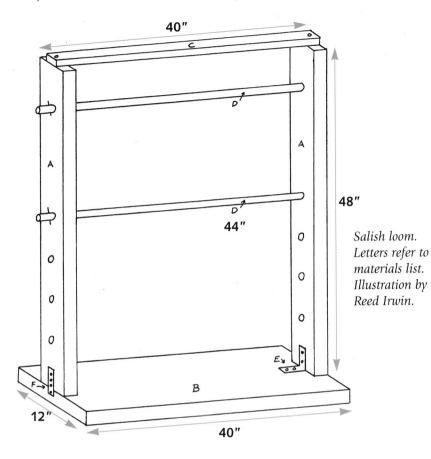

Salish loom. Letters refer to materials list. Illustration by Reed Irwin.

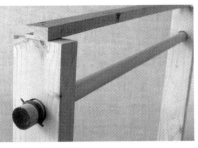

Detail of Salish loom showing top roller.

Salish Loom Materials

Reference Wood	Quantity	Size	Type/Description	Comments
A	1	2" x 4" x 8'	pine or fir	2 pieces 48" ea. (sides)
B	1	1" x 12" x 40"	pine or fir	base
C	2	1" x 2" x 40"	pine or fir	top brace
D	2	1-1/4"	closet rod or 1" dowels	cut 44" long (rollers)
Hardware				
E	2	3"	corner braces	with matching screws
F	2	4"	mending plates	with matching screws
	2	#8 x 1-1/2"	wood screws	
	4	6d x 1-3/4"	finishing nails	
	2	3mm x 36"	music wire	

OTHER EQUIPMENT

An **easel** or other support keeps a frame in a comfortable position. Choose a device that lets you rotate the frame. Some people prefer to hold a frame horizontally with one end supported on a table or chair. Employees at one nursing home clamp frames to tables to make them accessible to residents in wheelchairs.

Mechanical rag cutters make fabric preparation easy, but they are expensive, and some limit strip width. A **rotary fabric cutter**, used with a **cutting mat**, is an inexpensive alternative that can cut multiple thicknesses of fabric at once and reduces a woven fabric's tendency to ravel. Use a **ruler** to guide the cutter. An unthreaded serger will also cut fabric strips. Cutting strips by hand can wear out a pair of scissors quickly, especially when working with tough fabrics such as knits, and long cutting sessions are hard on the hands.

Tearing strips is a quick option for woven cloth, but it ravels the fabric, making it more difficult to work with. Some knitted fabrics (including nylon tricot) will tear in one direction without fraying; make sure it's the direction with least stretch (usually parallel to a selvedge). The edges of torn knits often curl inward, but not always in the direction you want. Tear fabric only in a well-ventilated place and for a short period of time, preferably with a dust mask; fabric dust (especially cotton) can be a health hazard. Dust and dirt are also problems when cutting and twining. Clean used fabrics before you start, to protect your health and to keep from dulling your cutter.

During twining, you will need **scissors, needles, thread** to match your fabrics, and a couple of **safety pins**. A sturdy **crochet hook** helps you poke the last rows of weft around the warp and to pull weft or warp ends through completed rows to hide them.

This frame clamps to a table and can be moved up and down to keep the twining at a comfortable level. Courtesy Judy Hughes.

*T*herapy programs and sheltered workshops have included rag twining for many years. At St. John's Home, a nursing facility in Milwaukee, twining is part of a crafts program for residents, many of whom are in their 90s when they learn the technique. Twining provides occupational therapy — keeping people busy rather than training them for employment — and it is also physical therapy. Residents are encouraged to tear rag strips, which provides gentle exercise. Twining helps improve manual dexterity, even for residents with severe arthritis.

More important, according to St. John's staff member Judy Hughes, is the spiritual and emotional therapy twining provides. A gift shop sells twined rugs and other crafts created by the residents and customers commission special orders. "Knowing they are working on rugs for particular customers gives our residents the incentive to get out of bed in the morning, to come downstairs and socialize with others," says Hughes. "Having goals helps keep their lives productive and promotes positive attitudes that benefit their physical as well as emotional health."

Esther Kelso (age 95) twines a rug at St. John's Home. Courtesy Judy Hughes, St. John's Home.

Rug twined by Esther Kelso. Collection of Bobbie Irwin.

WARP MATERIALS & PREPARATION

Fabric Vs. String Warp

Fabric warp makes a thick, dense rug that may be more durable than one with string or yarn warp. However, this dense structure is a disadvantage if a fabric warp becomes wet, because damp warp will not dry quickly and can rot or mildew, especially in humid climates. String or yarn warp dries faster than cloth and is a better choice for rugs frequently exposed to moisture, or for thin, lightweight rugs.

String warp should be strong, and for best results should be about as thick as a pencil; you can use multiple strands together. Avoid plastic baling twine, which may cause a rug to curl. String or yarn can be easier to work with than fabric, although hairy cord can irritate your fingers. String warps are sometimes easier to keep aligned than fabric warps when you twine the first rows. Plastic clothesline is thick, strong, impervious to moisture, and may be a sensible choice, although it is considerably more expensive than other warp materials. Like other warps, it shows slightly on the top and bottom edges of a rug, and its slippery quality makes it difficult to secure when a rug is finished.

Traditionally, most twined rugs had fabric warps, typically 1″-wide strips of sturdy, nonstretchy cloth such as denim, canvas, or pillow ticking. Because the warp is completely covered except at the top and bottom, it is protected from wear.

Because denim jeans have been universally available for a long time, especially in country homes where so many twined rugs were made, many old rugs have denim warp. It is strong and inelastic but it ravels, making it harder to work with than some other fabric warps. Raveled edges may show through on the surface if the weft is smooth or slick.

Nonraveling fabrics make

The raveled edges of a denim warp show on the surface of this tapestry rug, detracting from its appearance. Rug by Bobbie Irwin.

twining easier. Knits work well, stripped in the direction of least stretch. A little stretch in the warp is okay, but too much stretch may cause the ends of a rug to curl.

Warp Width

Strip any fabric warp so it compresses to about the diameter of a pencil. Since the warp is mostly covered, color is not particularly important and you can use different colors or different compatible fabrics in the same warp. However, unless you tie on a fringe or bind the ends with fabric, the warp *will* show at the top and bottom edges, so I usually use one of the same fabrics for warp that I use for weft in the top and bottom rows.

Warp Joins

To join fabric strips for warp, I recommend machine-sewing them. For a smooth join without bulk, overlap the ends at right angles, right sides together, sew across the diagonal, then trim the excess.

Warp strips joined with machine stitching.

Alternatively, you could use a serger, which trims the fabric automatically, or sew warp strips together by hand.

Many people prefer the ease and speed of an unsewn join,

even though it is bulkier and weaker than a sewn seam. There are two ways to join strips without sewing them. For the first method, cut small slits near the ends of two strips and overlap the ends, ends facing and slits aligned. Bring the opposite end of the top strip through both slits from the bottom and pull tight.

Overlap slits and pull one end through.

For the second method, pass the slit end of one strip through the slit on the second strip, then pass the opposite end of the second strip through the slit on the first strip ("old into new, new into old"). Pull tight.

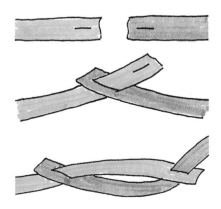

Pass one strand through the slit in the other, then the opposite end of the second strand through the slit in the first.

You can cut yardage in a spiral or cut almost through the fabric alternately from opposite sides to make continuous strips. I don't recommend spiral cuts for stretchy fabrics, since the changing orientation produces a strip with variable stretch. The second method creates extra bulk at the end of each cut, but it's not evident in the finished rug.

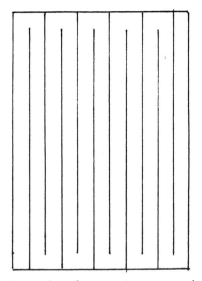

Cut yardage for a continuous strand.

Different fabrics in the same warp should be the same weight or cut so they compress to the same size (cut to balance). It's often easiest to cut with the grain of the fabric, although it's not necessary with nonstretchy fabrics, so you can salvage odd-shaped scraps. Bias-cut strips may have too much stretch.

To lengthen a string warp, tie on additional string. Splice or overlap and sew sections of heavy cord together. A little bulk at a warp join is usually not apparent in the finished rug.

How Much Warp Do I Need?

Estimate the amount of warp needed (in inches) by multiplying the number of warps per inch by the width of the rug by the length of the finished rug (in inches, including any excess warp to be left as fringe or woven in later). Divide by 12 to convert to feet, or by 36 for yards. This is relatively easy when warp spacing is predetermined on a pegged frame; otherwise, you must do a test with your fabric strips, twining a row or two on a sampler frame to determine the warp spacing. For example, let's say you plan to make a 30" x 54" rug and your test indicates a spacing of 2-1/2 warps per inch. Multiply 2-1/2 x 30" x 54". This gives you 75 warps (2-1/2 warps per inch x 30"), each 54" long, with a total warp length of 4,050". Dividing by 36 gives 112-1/2 yards and you'll need to allow a little extra for joining warp strips and securing the ends. For continuous warping, allow a little more warp than you think you'll need. Bulky warps require slightly more length than thin warps.

To determine how much cloth you need for fabric warp or weft, also consider the width of the strips. A yard of 45"-wide fabric will yield 45 yards of 1" strips, or 30 yards of 1-1/2"-wide strips. In the instructions, warp and weft yardages are the lengths of the strips, not the uncut fabric. The table below will help you estimate how many yards of strips a specific length of fabric will yield. Amounts are rounded *down* to the nearest full yard (if a certain yardage yields 4.7 yards of strips, the chart says 4 yards). In inches, divide the fabric width (or length) by the strip width, multiply by the fabric length (or width), and divide by 36 to estimate the number of yards of strips you can make. Always allow a little extra. Depending on fabric size, cutting selvedge-to-selvedge may yield more (or fewer) strips than cutting parallel to a selvedge. Cut in the direction of least stretch.

Fabric Width	Yardage	Strip Width in Inches								
		1	1-1/4	1-1/2	1-3/4	2	2-1/4	2-1/2	2-3/4	3
36"	1/4	9	7	6	5	4	4	3	3	3
36"	1/2	18	14	12	10	9	8	7	6	6
36"	3/4	27	21	18	15	13	12	10	9	9
36"	1	36	28	24	20	18	16	14	13	12
44"	1/4	11	8	7	6	4-5	4	3-4	3-4	3
44"	1/2	22	17	14	12	11	9	8	7-8	7
44"	3/4	33	25-26	21-22	18	15-16	14	12	11-12	10-11
44"	1	44	35	29	25	22	19	17	16	14
65"	1/4	16	12-13	10	9	7-8	7	5-6	5	5
65"	1/2	32	25-26	21	18	16	14	12-13	10-11	10
65"	3/4	48	37-39	32	27	23-24	21	18-19	16-17	15-16
65"	1	65	50-52	43	36-37	32	28	25-26	23	21

This table shows how many yards of strips a certain amount of fabric will yield, rounded down to the nearest full yard. Where there is a range of numbers, the direction you cut the fabric makes a difference. Cut fabric in the direction of the least stretch.

WEFT MATERIALS & PREPARATION

Choice of Fabric

Wefts must be flexible, since twining involves continual twisting. I don't recommend stiff or bulky fabric such as some upholstery or blanket material. Virtually any other fabric makes good weft, even sheer lightweight cloth. Although it's easiest to twine with wefts of the same type and weight, many successful rugs combine different fabrics.

A little stretch in the weft makes a nice tight rug, but if a fabric is extremely stretchy, selvedges may become distorted (especially if some of the weft is less elastic). This is especially true when working taaniko, which pulls wefts tight. Very stretchy fabrics are difficult to use successfully.

Because the weft fabric dominates, your choice of weft will determine the overall appearance, density, and feel of the finished rug. How will you use your rug? Does it need to be tough enough to clean muddy boots, or do you want it soft to cushion bare feet in a bathroom or bedroom? Will the rug be primarily decorative and not subject to hard use? Will it rest on a hard floor or on carpeting?

To complement an elegant interior, nylon tricot, satin, velour, and velvet are good choices. Strips of an old chenille bedspread or worn socks make a soft, textured rug (but not one for wiping muddy boots on). Denim is a good choice for an informal, country look (or for a rug that gets a lot of hard use). Crisp fabrics such as cotton broadcloth tend to make a rug with a firm surface. Many knits produce a soft, spongy feel. How tightly you twine will also influence the softness of a rug; the harder you pull, the firmer the rug will feel (and the longer it may last).

If safety is a major consideration, avoid slick fabric and choose a string warp to make a thin rug. (On the other hand, the heavier weight of a fabric-warp rug may help keep it in place.) Countered twining (see page 8) is important to keep edges from curling. Rubber or canvas mats under scatter rugs help keep them from sliding, and any sort of padding prolongs the life of a rug.

Fabrics that ravel are harder to work with and may leave loose threads on the surface, which gradually disappear with use and cleaning. Knit fabrics don't usually ravel; woven fabrics will. Fabrics with fine, firmly packed threads ravel less than loosely woven cloth.

Laundering new fabrics before twining removes sizing and makes them more flexible. Although shrinkage is not usually a problem unless a rug is machine-washed, laundering the cloth before you cut it preshrinks it and helps remove excess dye that might "bleed" onto other colors when you clean a rug. I wash wool fabrics using hot water, cold rinse, and the normal cycles of my washer and dryer. This shrinks and felts them, making them less prone to ravel, and tightens the fabric structure for a longer-lasting rug. If you don't want to use this sort of shock treatment, cutting wool fabrics on the bias may reduce raveling and the extra stretch is not a problem in the weft.

Weft Width

Ideal weft width is a matter of personal preference. The narrower the strips, the thinner your rug will be and the more rows and time it will require for completion. I twine tightly, and most of my rugs have a warp and weft spacing between 2-1/2 and three rows per inch. This is close enough to twine intricate patterns in a reasonable time period. I have seen thin rugs with as many as seven rows per inch, made from lightweight fabric cut less than 1" wide. (One nursing home deliberately uses narrow wefts to keep its residents busy longer!) For a thick rug that works up quickly, use heavy, wide fabric strips. If you plan to sell your rugs, this may be your best choice.

The widths for the projects in this book reflect my own preferences but are fairly standard. I usually cut weft strips so they compress to about the diameter of a pencil. Scrunch or roll a corner of the fabric somewhat loosely to estimate the width you need. Before cutting your entire fabric supply, sample a couple rows (a small sampler frame is ideal for this). If the weft doesn't cover the warp adequately or pulls the sides in, try again with a wider strip (often a 1/4″ change is adequate). If the weft seems too bulky and distorts the warp outward, cut the next strip narrower. Changing warp width and spacing are other options.

Careful sampling is important when using more than one type or weight of fabric together, especially with tapestry or taaniko. The widths you choose are less important than *balancing* the wefts — making sure they compress to the same size so they are compatible. When you use a heavy fabric with a lighter one, you must cut the heavier weft narrower. If your supply of a fabric is limited, sampling helps determine how much a project requires at different widths, then you can cut the more abundant fabrics to balance.

Cut heavy wefts such as denim and heavy wool as narrow as 1″. Cut lighter-weight fabrics wider. For example, if you cut corduroy 1-1/2″ wide,

cotton broadcloth might need to be 2″ to 3″ wide, and sheer fabrics 3″ to 4″ wide. The same type of fabric can come in different weights, which need to be cut in different widths. With a little experience, you will soon develop a feel for the proper widths to achieve the results you want.

How Much Weft Do I Need?

Twining uses up a lot of fabric, especially when both warp and weft are cloth; a 2′ x 3′ rug can weigh five pounds. In my experience, a rug with fabric warp needs about four times as much weft as warp.

Calculate the linear feet in a rug by multiplying the width in inches by the number of rows you anticipate and dividing by 12. (The number of rows is the number of weft rows per inch — determined by sampling — times the length of the rug in inches.) In regular twining, a foot of row requires two wefts, each about 2′ long. Three-weft twining uses approximately

equal amounts of three strips, almost half a yard of each to twine a foot of row. Taaniko uses much more of the dominant weft (the one that shows) than of the hidden weft; each linear foot in which a single color is exposed requires a little more than 36″ of the dominant weft and 1′ of the hidden weft. Your requirements may vary, so be sure to sample. While heavier fabrics or wider strips require fewer rows, their extra bulk may require more length to cover a certain distance.

If you have limited amounts of a weft fabric and want a symmetrically balanced pattern, divide your weft into equal piles, one for each half of the rug. When your supply runs out on one end of the rug, you'll have enough to twine the equivalent amount on the other end.

Fabric Patterns & Colors

This old Nuu-chah-nulth rug features a delightful pattern of canoes and seabirds. Beneath the boats, blue cloth alternates with a lighter-colored fabric, giving the effect of waves on the ocean. Close examination reveals clusters of tiny white dots on the blue cloth, like seafoam on the waves. Although the effect is visible only on close inspection, I'm sure it was deliberate. I can imagine the rugmaker smiling with satisfaction when she found just the right cloth (or perhaps she found it first and used it as in-

These fabrics are "cut to balance," ranging from 1″ to 2-1/4″ wide. Left to right: denim, wool, corduroy, heavy knit, medium knit, cotton broadcloth, jersey.

spiration for her design).

Choosing fabrics for special effects is an exciting part of rug twining. The texture of the cloth — shiny, crisp, soft, tough, or ribbed — influences a rug's appearance and feel. Striped, plaid, and printed fabrics produce a variety of effects, depending partly on how you cut them. Plaids produce pleasing hit-and-miss effects as different colors appear on the surface. Twining compresses fabrics and can subdue their original flamboyance. Large, bold prints work better than tiny calico patterns, which may get lost during twining.

Weft strips you use together can be different compatible fabrics. Different patterns

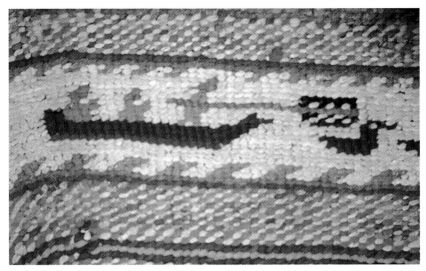

Detail of a Nuu-chah-nulth twined rag rug from the Mary McNeill Sieburth Collection. Catalogue #18707, Royal British Columbia Museum. Courtesy Linda Heinrich, Kelowna, British Columbia.

might "fight" with each other, so you may prefer a solid-colored weft with a patterned one. Using distinct fabrics makes it easier to see errors, especially when you are learning. (On the other hand, a jumble of patterns or colors will camouflage mistakes if you don't like to correct them!)

Plaid fabric produces an interesting color pattern in this small rug by Bobbie Irwin.

Large areas twined in a solid color accentuate weft joins, soiling, and uneven selvedges. Static electricity in nylon attracts dust; solid-colored nylon shows dirt more readily than some other fabrics. Dark colors may disguise soil better than light colors, although "dirt-colored" fabrics also work well. I have seen one old rug made entirely from white sheets — not a very practical choice.

Pictorial rugs are wonderful exercises for your imagination. Try tweeds for mottled backgrounds; herringbone weaves for feathers; velvet, chenille, or velour for fluffy clouds. Shiny satin and nylon tricot evoke sunlight reflecting off a surface; dark velour makes convincing shadows. A printed cotton may produce just the right variegation for leaves on a tree; consider moire´ fabric for ripples on water. Be aware that subtle textures and patterns usually look different in a rug than on flat yardage and may not give the effects you expect.

Sources for Fabrics

Old rugs were truly made from rags. When I enthusiastically showed Lillie Sherwood the nylon tricot I'd purchased for twining, she reminded me that the tradition is to use what you have. "It's nice," she agreed, "but honey, you *bought* that." She herself bought second-hand clothing to tear up for rugs and she used scraps of new fabric from her daughter's business; still, this was part of the tradition of using cast-off clothing and remnants. Lillie bought new corduroy for her last rug, to get just the color she needed, but that was an exception to her thrifty nature.

Quilting has a similar tradition, yet modern quilters can choose from a vast array of fabrics designed specifically for them. And who is to say that quilters and rug twiners 100 years ago didn't buy new fabrics now and then for their creations, or at least choose a dress fabric with an eye toward its second life? You needn't feel guilty about buying new materials for twining. A rug is as legitimate a use as any for new fabric, and buying brand-new material may bring less guilt than cutting up good clothing that someone else could wear.

On the other hand, a rug with familiar fabric can have special significance. When I purchased a rug made by Willis Leenhouts at St. John's Home in Milwaukee, staff members said the rug, twined from his old bathrobe, evoked fond memories of him.

My rugs often combine new cloth (usually remnants) with recycled clothing. Some rug designs require considerable amounts of a single fabric not normally available except by the yard. However, used sheets, bedspreads, blankets, draperies, and slipcovers supply considerable amounts of cloth at little cost, and comparable new materials might be quite expensive. An old velveteen or satin curtain is a bonanza, especially if it is lined with a second usable fabric! Fading or stains often won't matter in a rug, or you can work around them.

Long velour robes are a wonderful source for rich-looking rug fabrics. I typically salvage 50 to 80 yards of weft strips from an old bathrobe. A

Rag rug makers may have been the original recyclers. Resourceful people have probably converted their worn fabrics into rugs for centuries, yet there are few examples known from before 1800.

One reason there are few very old rag rugs is that they were made from old materials to begin with, and they were made for heavy use. Even old rugs were recycled. When the warp on a loom-woven rug disintegrated, the rag strips might be rewoven into a new rug. Rugs too shabby for the floor found extended life in the barn, doghouse, or tool shed. Rag rugs were rarely if ever intended as heirlooms to pass down to another generation, and most didn't end up in museums where they could be preserved.

pair of blue jeans yields 30 to 50 yards of 1"-wide strips, depending on the garment size. It's faster to discard seams and pockets rather than to try to salvage every inch of fabric, but save the scraps in case you end up needing just a little more.

Textile mills and clothing factories are good sources of remnants and selvedge strips, which sometimes come already cut and rolled in suitable widths, at little or no cost. If companies near you do not advertise remnants, inquire; they may be happy to give you scraps they might otherwise discard. A few businesses strip and sell industrial remnants, and some will cut them to your specifications at reasonable cost, saving you preparation time.

Weft Joins

While a fabric warp is often a continuous piece, weft strips need to be shorter, no more than a couple yards long. The twisting action of twining requires wefts short enough to be continually manipulated to the front and back sides of a rug. I rarely work with weft strips longer than two yards. Taaniko uses up the surface weft more quickly, and since the dominant color stays on top, you can use strips up to four yards long. If you insist on working with long strips, bunch up the ends and secure them with rubber bands to keep them manageable.

Unless weft scraps are very short, you needn't sew them together ahead of time. Add weft extensions as you twine. Overlap strips about 1", fold edges inward, and use a few quick whipstitches with matching thread to join the wefts and tack down the loose edge. Tapering one or both weft strips at the join reduces bulk.

Overlap weft ends.

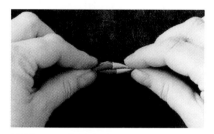
Fold raw edges in.

Sew strips together.

Slit joins (see page 25) are an option for twiners who have difficulty manipulating or threading a needle (or who just refuse to sew!). Slit joins are more difficult to position precisely for patterning. Hand-

sewing wefts together on the diagonal is more time-consuming and weaker than overlapping strips, and while it reduces bulk, the diagonal join is not always suitable for pattern changes.

Fabric glue is a possible alternative. However, glue may slow your progress while it dries, some adhesives may dissolve when you clean a rug, and glue can speed fabric deterioration. You can hold overlapped wefts together without joining them, until both ends are securely twined, but not when a pattern requires a join at a selvedge.

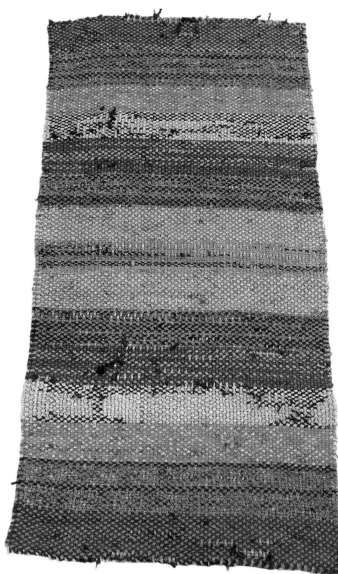

Rug by Fred Schroer, 1895-1978, owned by his grand-niece, Judy Aurelius, Royalton, Minnesota.

Wool rug by Willis Leenhouts. Collection of Bobbie Irwin.

My mom's uncle died before I knew weaving was part of me. Uncle Fred made twined rugs. He made some for my mom from an old couch cover we had when I was little. It's like a quilt with a piece of your old dress — nice, vague memories.

Judy Aurelius

Chapter 3

Learning to Twine

WARPING

There are many warping methods, each with advantages and disadvantages. Some methods are more appropriate for certain projects or equipment than others, so it's useful to know several techniques, even if you use only one most of the time. Following are descriptions of the most common methods; you are welcome to use your own adaptations. The same techniques apply to string and fabric warps.

Method #1:
Continuous Warp

Sew fabric strips together for a continuous warp or use a long piece of string. The technique is easiest on a pegged frame; the bulk of a fabric warp is tricky to manipulate around wires. Adjust each strand so tension is even but not as tight as possible.

On a Pegged Frame: Start at one corner (traditionally the upper left) and loop about 3″ of warp around the first peg, pinning it in place temporarily.

Zigzag the warp onto the frame. Each length between the top and bottom pegs is one warp.

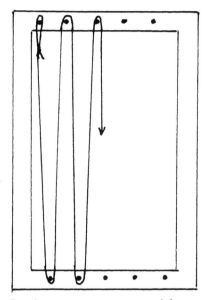

Continuous warp on a pegged frame. The traditional method fastens the start of the warp to the same strand.

If you sew the ends to the selvedge warps, be careful when you remove a rug from the frame, because the wefts could easily slip off those warps. Immediately sew the weft to the warp in the corners where the warp starts and ends. Sewing the ends to the *adjacent*

warps eliminates the need for finishing. When you twine, treat overlapped ends as part of the warps they are sewn to.

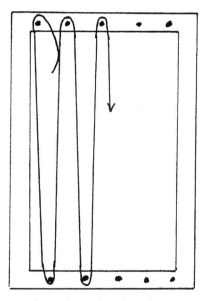

Attaching the end to the adjacent strand is recommended.

On an Unpegged Frame: Wrap a continuous warp around the ends of a plain frame for a rug with warp that serves as fringe. Figure-eight warping will help keep strands in order. Bring the warp through the center of the frame on each circuit.

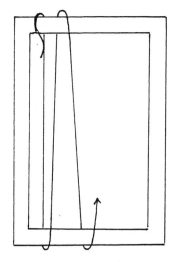

Continuous warp around an unpegged frame. Warp passes through the center on each pass.

Remove crossbars or cut the warps to remove the rug from the frame. If you leave warp as fringe, sew the top and bottom rows of weft to the warp all the way across, to keep them from slipping. If you prefer, hide warps by pulling the ends back into the rug.

On a Frame With Suspended Wires: Use figure-eight warping. Keep the wires parallel and the desired distance apart while adjusting tension.

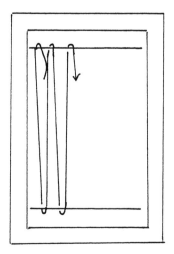

Continuous warp around suspended wires (support for the wires is not shown).

On a Frame With Rollers: *Reverse warping* makes a rug with four finished edges, up to twice as long as the distance between the dowels. Wrap the warp around a wire slightly shorter than the inside width of the frame. Temporarily tie the wire about 8″ down from and parallel to the top dowel.

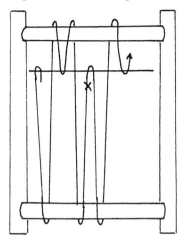

Reverse warping around a single wire. The warp does not cross through the center of the frame. For clarity, the strands are shown separated; attach the start of the warp to the adjacent warp at the X.

Remove the ties when the warp is in place and properly tensioned. The wire and warp rotate around the frame as you work.

For a shorter rug, use reverse warping around two wires tied together. Loop the end of the warp around the wire, pinning it temporarily. Pass the warp in circular fashion around the bottom roller, over the top roller, and back to the wire. Wrap the warp around the wire and reverse directions — over the top roller, then around the bottom roller. Each time the warp returns to the wire, wrap it around the wire and reverse

directions; don't bring the warp through the center of the frame. A single warp travels all the way around the frame, wire to wire. If the first warp goes around the bottom roller first, ending the warp by coming up from the bottom gives an even number of warps; ending by coming down from the top gives an odd number. Sew warp ends to the adjacent warps. Pull out the wire(s) when the rug is finished.

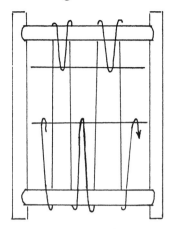

Reverse warping around two wires, for shorter rugs. The wires are tied together (not shown).

Method #2: Warp Loops

Sew or tie double lengths of warp into loops that serve as two warps; allow a little extra (the width of the warp) for sewing the overlap on the diagonal. Sew a wide piece of fabric into a tube and cut the tube into warp loops. For an odd number of warps, sew an individual strand to the adjacent warp or fasten it to the frame temporarily and pull in the ends when a rug is finished. Warp loops are much quicker to put on a frame than a continuous warp, which requires tension adjustments.

On a Pegged Frame: Slip the loops over the pegs; position the joins away from the top and bottom where they would show.

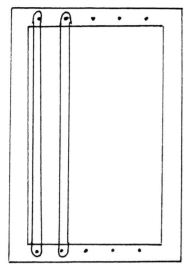

Warp loops on a pegged frame.

On an Unpegged Frame: Sew or tie loops directly onto a frame. Alternate twining around warps from the front and back.

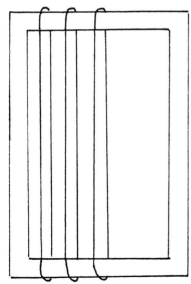

Warp loops on a plain frame.

On a Frame With Suspended Wires: With the frame upright, place the loops on the top wire, adding supports at regular intervals. Then slip the bottom wire through the loops, with supports, and tension the wires. If the loops are the same length, the wires should be parallel. Position joins away from the wires.

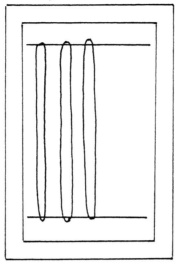

Warp loops on suspended wires. Supports for the wires are not shown

On a Frame With Rollers: With reverse warping, each end of a loop goes around the wire. Don't pass the warp through the center of the frame.

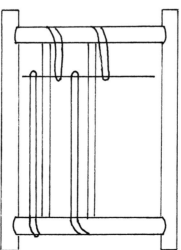

Reverse warping with looped warps.

Method #3: Individual Warps

This is an unusual variation except for curved rugs. It saves preparation time and gives you the option of odd or even numbers, but is slower to put on a frame.

On a Pegged or Unpegged Frame: Tie or tack on separate warps with the same tension.

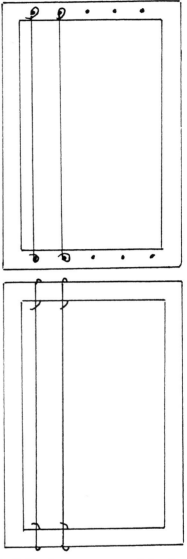

Individual warps on pegged (top) or unpegged (bottom) frames.

On a Hoop: Tie or tack strands onto the rim; it's easier than a continuous warp. Each strand across the diameter serves as two warps; add more as you twine. Start with just a few warps to minimize bulk where they cross at the center.

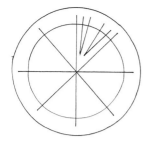

Tack or tie radiating warps onto a circular hoop. Add additional warps in pairs as you twine (upper right).

On an oval hoop, warps across the narrower dimension should be parallel to each other, straight up and down. Add radiating warps at the sides as you work; these do not extend to the center.

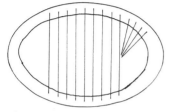

Tack parallel warps on an oval hoop; add radiating warps at the sides as you twine (upper right).

Without a Frame: For a circular rug, cross a few strands at the center; you may tack them together to keep them from slipping as you start twining. Add more as you work outwards, folding a strip in half to make a new pair. Start an oval rug with parallel warps, taping or tacking them down temporarily if you wish. Add radiating warps at the sides when you start twining in a continuous spiral.

*N*ate Jones, a Utah twiner, never uses a frame for his circular, rectangular, and oval rugs. He starts rectangular and oval rugs by cutting parallel slits in a solid piece of fabric, using this fringe as the warp. After twining one side, he cuts slits for the opposite side. Sometimes Nate cuts additional warps perpendicular to the first for working an adjacent side. To start a circular rug, he holds overlapped and radiating warps in his hand.

Warp Tension

On a frame, keep tension on the warp even and fairly tight, but not as tight as possible. Tension increases as you twine, especially with bulky materials.

If a warp loosens or breaks while twining, sew a tuck in a fabric warp or overlap and sew broken ends. Sew, knot, or splice a string warp. Extra bulk doesn't normally show in a finished rug.

An Odd or Even Number of Warps?

Most striped, hit-and-miss, and three-weft rugs don't require a specific number of warps, except to achieve a desired width. Either an odd or an even number will work. More complex patterns may require a certain number of warps for symmetry.

Tapestry designs require an odd or even number, depending on the join, the number of pattern blocks, and the number of warps in the blocks (see

Tapestry Join	# of Blocks	Total Warps in Blocks	Shared Warps	Total Warps
dovetailed	even	even	odd	odd
dovetailed	even	odd	odd	even
dovetailed	odd	even	even	even
dovetailed	odd	odd	even	odd
interlocked	even	even	none	even
interlocked	even	odd	none	odd
interlocked	odd	even	none	even
interlocked	odd	odd	none	odd

Calculate whether you need an odd or even number of warps for twined tapestry. Total warps in pattern blocks (column 3) does not include any shared warps between blocks.

the table on page 36). Most designs that are worked from a graphed pattern need a specific number of warps.

Warp loops give an even number, but other warping methods let you choose an odd or even number of warps. A continuous warp that ends in the corner diagonally opposite from where you started will have an odd number. A warp that ends on the opposite side of the same crossbar is even.

When Do I Have Enough Warps?

Unless your pattern dictates otherwise, you can add or subtract warps after you sample a row or two. If you've used all the pegs on a frame, you can't add more warps, but you can use fewer. On an unpegged frame, you can add or subtract warps.

Don't secure the end of a warp permanently until you've twined one or two rows to check for warp coverage and distortion. Make sure you have enough warps before cutting off excess. Instead of changing the number of warps, you can change weft width or twining tension. Especially when color changes are frequent, a complex pattern may require more width than an unpatterned background. Sample a test pattern to determine the proper number of warps, even if the actual pattern doesn't really start on the first row, then twine more loosely in background rows.

GENERAL TWINING INSTRUCTIONS

These are general instructions only. Specific instructions are included with the samplers (pages 41 to 78) and projects (pages 80 to 111). Read through these general directions before you start working on a specific project.

Twining is neither a right- nor a left-handed activity. Both hands do the work and because the direction usually reverses with each row, the hands swap tasks. Although one direction may feel more awkward at first, you will soon become accustomed to working both directions.

It is traditional to twine from the top down on an upright frame, starting at the upper left corner. Once you are proficient, choose any method that is comfortable and gives satisfactory results.

Start at least 1″ down from the pegs or wires and move weft rows upward to fill the gap after you've twined a row or two. To pack weft rows together at any stage, tug on the warp, rather than pushing weft rows, except on a curved rug. Hold the last row in place with one hand while you pull down on the warp with the other.

Treat overlapped warp ends as part of the warps they're sewn to. Otherwise, consider each strand as a single warp — unless using multiple strands of string, where you treat a group as a single warp. Twine

each warp in the same order it was placed on the frame, without allowing warps to cross. On a frame with rollers, keep front and back warp layers separate.

For most twining variations, it's customary to work from both ends, rotating the frame occasionally. The terms *top* and *up* refer to whichever end of the frame is up at a particular time; the *top* of a horizontal frame is the end farthest away from you. Mark the front side of a plain frame so you will remember which side you were working on.

How Long Does It Take?

Since twining is hand-manipulated, it isn't quick. A complex pattern with three warps and rows per inch takes me four to five hours per square foot. Production speed depends on rug size, how tightly you twine, fabric widths and bulk, pattern complexity, and preparation time. A few rug-makers have created rugs in a day with relatively wide fabric strips and few rows per inch. Many twiners keep rugs on their frames for weeks. Twining doesn't require long work sessions; you can pick up again easily where you left off.

Weft Length & Joins

Except when a pattern requires specific color placement, stagger weft lengths so that joins don't fall in the same place. When both wefts are the same color at the start of a rug, fold a single strand so the ends are uneven.

As you use up wefts, attach additional strips as needed. Unless a pattern requires it, avoid joins at a selvedge, where they are visible and subject to wear. Hide joins between weft segments or on the backside of a rug to keep them inconspicuous.

Attach a new weft while there is still enough of the old one to work with. To sew a join at a desired spot, twine up to where you want the new weft to start, cut the old weft there, and untwine a few segments to fasten on the new strand. If sewing, enclose the new strip within the old strip.

Twining in Various Directions

My instructions assume you start at the upper left corner and twine across to the right side for the first row, with a left pitch (see page 8). If you prefer to start at the upper right cor-

ner, the weft segments in the first row should have a right pitch. Either way, twist toward the open warp and away from the top of the frame; this packs the rows more tightly than using the opposite twist.

You may prefer to work from the bottom of a rug upwards, especially on a horizontal frame or loom. To adapt the instructions, exchange "left" with "right" and "top" or "up" with "bottom" or "down," and turn the diagrams upside down. The twist direction should still be toward the untwined warp (top of the frame). Commence twining from the lower right corner with a left pitch.

If you start at the top from right to left, interchange the instructions for even- and odd-numbered rows. If you twine sideways, turn the diagrams on their sides. Any new technique will feel awkward until you are familiar with it; to avoid confusion, start by following the instructions as given.

Working From Both Ends

It makes good sense to twine from both ends of a rug toward the center. It's easiest to end a rug away from the edges of a frame and to keep the working area at a convenient height. Rotate the frame (top to bottom, not front to back) so you can continue to work downward; start the other end with two new wefts. If a pattern requires an even number of rows, start the other end in the upper *right* corner with a *right* pitch after you rotate the frame; otherwise, start at the upper left just as you did before.

When you use the same two weft colors on each end of a symmetrical rug, note which color goes on top of the selvedge after you rotate a frame. It depends on whether you have an odd or an even number of warps and need an odd or an even number of weft rows. Consult the chart below to be sure your patterns and

# Warps	# Rows	Starting Point	Pitch	Opposite Starting Point	Pitch	Start Opposite End with (Color on Top)
odd	odd	upper left	left	left	left	same color
odd	odd	upper right	right	right	right	same color
odd	even	upper left	left	right	right	different color
odd	even	upper right	right	left	left	different color
even	odd	upper left	left	left	left	different color
even	odd	upper right	right	right	right	different color
even	even	upper left	left	right	right	different color
even	even	upper right	right	left	left	different color

Determine twining directions and corner colors when working from both ends of a frame.

the countered twining come out the way you want them. It can be very frustrating to get to the last few rows and discover you should have started at the other side or with the other color on top!

Twining a row or two on each end at the start secures the warps in parallel order and provides a quick check for crossed warps. Pass your fingers up and down between them. If you encounter an obstruction, determine the proper order and correct the problem on one end or the other. Also check for missed warps or two twined together. It's much better to discover and correct these situations at an early stage than to try to compensate on the last rows of a rug.

The only type of rug I work completely in one direction, top to bottom, is a three-weft rug. The more complex interaction of three wefts makes it difficult to balance the pattern working from both ends. Any rug twined on a standard loom is best worked in one direction.

Finishing a Rug

It's neither necessary nor always desirable to finish your rug exactly in the middle. End in a row without a lot of patterning. After twining both ends of a rug, I sometimes work an entire pattern from one end before finishing near the other end of the warp. Whenever possible, end a rug within a row, rather than at a selvedge.

Except on curved or other same-pitch rugs, you normally need to maintain countered twining down to the final row. Sometimes you may no longer be able to see the warp, but you will need to force in another row to get the correct pitch or to make a pattern come out even. Use a blunt object to punch the weft through, if necessary. The last rows always take longer than other rows.

You usually end up with two wefts coming from each direction. Sew like ends together to form the last weft segments — two wefts on the front side and two on the back. Cut a small slit near the end of each weft and use a crochet hook through the slit to pull each weft end alongside a different warp for at least 1″, hiding it within several weft rows. A slick weft may need extra anchoring. Cut off the excess.

Particularly in tapestry, you may have to secure loose ends at the conclusion of a pattern area before you come to the last row of a rug. Sew them together and force them through previous rows, parallel to the warps, as you do when finishing a rug.

Some rugs come off their

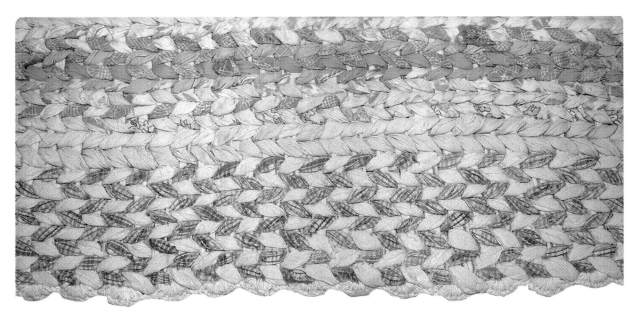

A crocheted edge finish on a rug twined in the 1930s by Sophia Jacobsen of Schleswig, Iowa. Collection of Lois Fronk, Fort Collins, Colorado.

frames ready to use and others need some finishing to secure the wefts. If you sew the ends of the warp to adjacent warps or use warp loops, no finishing is usually needed if you've twined right up to the ends of the warp. Whenever the first and last rows of weft might slip off one or more warps, sew the weft to the warp.

An edge finish is an option on any type of rug. You can crochet a decorative edge or add a fabric binding. A few old rugs have a braided edge. Edge finishes can prolong the life of a rug, since the edges are most susceptible to wear.

To fringe a rug, knot together two or more warps at the edge of a rug to secure the weft rows, or tie on fabric or yarn fringe using a lark's-head knot. Although fringe wears out faster than the rest of a rug, it's easy to replace.

Lark's-head knot.

Twining Large Rugs

A pegged frame with wide crossbars or a frame with rollers lets you make rugs wider or longer than the frame itself, and long rugs are possible on a standard floor loom. Few people ever twined rugs larger than 3' x 6'. You can sew together small rugs to make larger rugs, although stitching creates a weak zone where the sections can come apart eventually. You can take a sewn rug apart deliberately for easier cleaning. A few rugs have been made in sections, with new wefts sewn or looped onto old ones at a selvedge.

LEARNING BY SAMPLING

You may be anxious to start a full-sized rug, but take a little time to practice a technique before you commit a lot of time and fabric to a project. A method that looks appealing may prove more difficult or less suited to your purpose than you'd like, and it's better to find that out before you start a large rug! Making potholders on a small frame is an excellent way to learn pattern, warping, and equipment variations. A small frame is handy for sampling fabric widths and determining how much fabric you will need for a rug.

These samplers will give you all the experience you need to make rugs. Each introduces new challenges, materials, and design techniques. If you haven't twined before, start with Sampler #1, which introduces the basics, before you attempt more challenging techniques. Instructions for subsequent samplers assume this basic knowledge. Yardages refer to the combined length of fabric strips and are approximate.

See Chapter 2 for sampler frame instructions. Use similar types and weights of fabrics if possible, choosing your own patterns and colors. This will help you judge which fabrics you prefer, and you will have a set of reference samples. Even with the same types of fabric, you may have to cut your strips slightly different widths than I did to get similar results. Cut wefts so they balance, and test fabric widths before cutting the entire fabric supply.

Warps on the sides of a rug or sampler are *selvedges*. The *first warp* is usually a selvedge, but it can also be the first warp in a particular pattern area. The *second warp* is next to the selvedge (or pattern edge) — the second warp in from the left side, if you're working left to right, or from the right side, if you're working right to left. Similarly, I count other warps from the side you are working *from*.

REGULAR TWINING

Regular twining can produce a variety of patterns, depending on how many colors you use and how the wefts turn around the selvedges. Regular twining is easiest to learn using two distinct wefts that are compatible in color, such as one solid and one patterned fabric, which will alternate on the surface.

Fasten together two weft strips of unequal length. Position the join at the upper left corner with one weft on top of the selvedge and the other underneath. Bring the weft that is underneath back to the surface between the first two warps, headed toward the right, and slightly above the other weft without crossing it. A weft that goes under a warp always comes back to the surface.

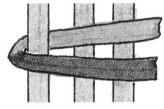

Start twining.

Take the weft that's on top of the selvedge down towards the bottom of the frame, under the second warp, then back to the surface between the second and third warps, extending toward the right.

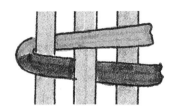

Create the first weft segment.

Cross the other weft over the first weft, top to bottom between the second and third warps, keeping it on top of the second warp. Pass it under the third warp and back to the surface.

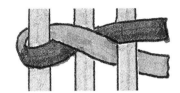

The second weft segment.

Continue all the way across, always working with the weft that's farthest behind (in the direction you are working from). You don't have to think about twisting — crossing the wefts forms the half twist that characterizes regular twining. Once a weft comes to the surface, it automatically lies on top of the next warp, so you just place it underneath the warp that follows. If you have trouble remembering which way to cross the wefts, put the weft you just took under a warp up over the top of the frame, out of the way.

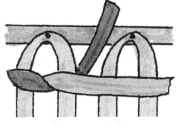

Put the weft up out of the way.

Pass the other weft under the next warp, then back to the surface.

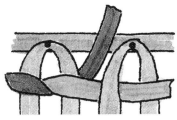

Slip the second weft under the next warp.

Put that weft strip up over the top of the frame, to the right of the first one without crossing them.

Both wefts out of the way; resume twining with the weft on the left.

Pass the first weft under the next warp. The twist and proper pitch should happen automatically.

Twine across to the right selvedge; each weft segment should slant to the left (left pitch).

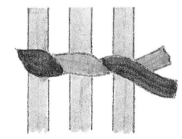

Left-pitch twining.

The colors should alternate horizontally and you should have as many weft segments as you have warps. If the color alternation or the pitch changes, make a correction. Make sure you have enclosed each warp separately, in order.

To turn around the right selvedge, take the weft that's on top of the selvedge behind the other weft *and* the selvedge warp, then back to the surface between the selvedge and adjacent warps.

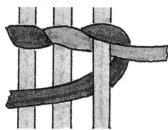

Start the turn.

Then take the other weft — the one underneath the selvedge on the first row — and bring it over the selvedge, down toward the bottom of the frame and under the second warp.

Turn with the second weft.

Continue twining toward the left.

Twine right to left.

The twisting motion is the same as when you are working the opposite direction, always crossing wefts top to bottom toward the bottom of the frame, but the pitch will automatically be *right* instead of left when you are working from right to left.

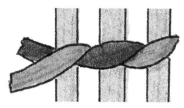

Right-pitch twining.

Weft colors should alternate vertically as well as horizontally, producing a checkerboard pattern that helps you check for errors. If the pattern or pitch changes in a row, make a correction where the change occurred.

Turn around the left selvedge the same way as at the right; start with the weft that's on top of the selvedge, then take the other weft around.

Turn at the left.

Complete the turn.

Weft segments in odd-numbered rows should have a left pitch. The pattern is the same for an odd or even number of warps.

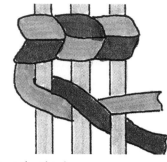

Start the third row.

A simple edge-turn variation lines up the weft colors vertically. Twine from left to right as described above. The weft on top of the selvedge crosses behind the other weft but stays on top of the selvedge to start the next row.

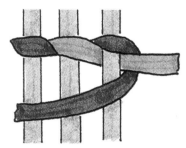

Keep the same color on the selvedge.

The other weft goes under the selvedge, coming back to the surface between the selvedge and second warp.

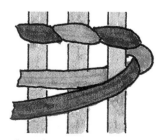

Complete the turn.

The weft on top of the selvedge then goes down and under the second warp.

Start the second row; colors line up vertically.

Pull the weft that's underneath the selvedge a little tighter until it doesn't show on the edge. Twining from right to left is the same as in the checkerboard variation; the colors line up vertically and alternate horizontally.

Turn at the left selvedge the same way as at the right; the color on top of the selvedge on one row stays on top to start the next row, and the weft beneath the selvedge stays under it on the next row. Except for the edge turn, the twining method and pitch directions remain the same. An odd number of warps will give symmetrical vertical stripes; with an even number, you end up with a different color on each selvedge.

Because of the random color order in a hit-and-miss rug, you may get the checkerboard effect in some areas and a vertical stripe effect in others, no matter which edge turn you use.

For horizontal stripes, use the same fabric for both wefts, with joins at the selvedges and consistent pitch. There's no color contrast to check accuracy.

Hit-and-miss rug started by Lillie Sherwood and completed by Bobbie Irwin.

Countered Twining, Solid Stripes, and Edge-Turn Variations

Use this sampler to master regular countered twining and simple pattern variations for reversible rugs. Sewing warp ends to the selvedge warps provides a comparison with the preferred method in most other samplers.

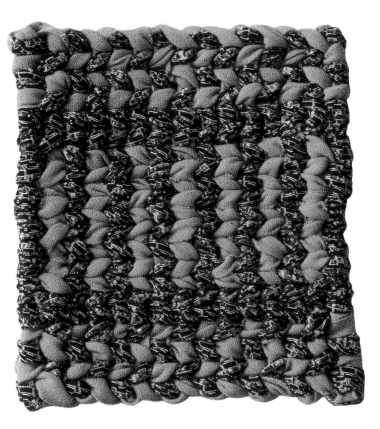

Frame: Pegged sampler frame.

Warping Method: Continuous.

Warp: Medium-weight knit fabric, 3-1/2 yards 1-1/4″ wide. Use one of the same fabrics you will use for weft (I used the solid color).

Weft: Medium-weight knit fabric: 8-1/2 yards of patterned fabric 1-1/4″ wide, 5 yards of solid fabric 1-1/4″ wide. Fabrics should be the same weight and width.

Fabric samples; the warp (also used for weft) is on the left.

Warping: Wrap the end of the warp around the first nail in the upper left corner, overlap about 3", and sew down the end, forming a loop.

Sew the end to the first warp.

Zigzag the warp back and forth from top to bottom, ending in the lower right with 15 warps. Keep the warp taut but not extremely tight.

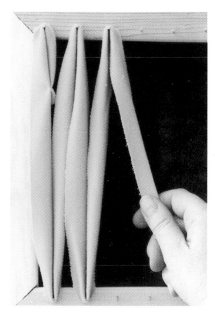

Zigzag the warp between nails.

Overlap the end around the last nail, and pin temporarily without cutting off the excess.

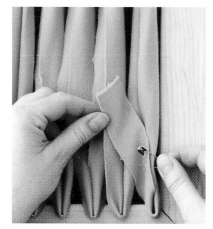

Pin the end temporarily.

Twining: Fasten together a strip of each fabric, of unequal lengths (two yards maximum). Starting about 1" down from the nails, place the patterned weft on top of the first warp at the upper left, with the solid weft underneath. Bring the solid weft back to the surface between the first two warps, slightly above the patterned weft, enclosing the overlapped end of the first warp.

Start twining.

Take the patterned weft down toward the bottom of the frame, under the second warp, and back to the surface.

The first weft segment.

Cross the solid weft over the patterned weft between the first and second warps, top to bottom, over the second warp, and under the third warp, below the patterned weft.

The second weft segment.

Continue across, using each weft in turn and maintaining a left pitch, with colors alternating. Always cross the wefts toward the untwined warp, top to bottom, not toward the previous row.

At the right selvedge, take the weft on top (patterned) behind the solid weft, under the edge warp, and back to the surface between the first two warps.

Start the turn.

Bring the solid weft over the selvedge, below the patterned weft, under the second warp, and back to the surface.

The completed turn.

Twine as before, right to left, with a right pitch. Colors should alternate both horizontally and vertically.

If the colors line up instead of alternating, you may have twined two warps together, skipped a warp, or turned incorrectly. If the pitch changes within a row, you crossed the wefts in the wrong direction. If

Start the second row; right-pitch twining.

a weft segment has no obvious pitch, you neglected to cross the wefts. Untwine and make corrections.

If the warp is distorted, decide if you need to cut weft strips wider or narrower, or untwine and remove two warps on the right side (to keep an odd number). When you are satisfied with the number of warps and the weft widths, push the weft up against the nails. Remove the pin, sew the end to the last warp, and trim the excess.

Move the rows up by pulling the warp.

Rotate the frame and start the other end with two new wefts, starting with the pat-

terned strip on top of the selvedge. After twining a row, run your fingers up and down between warps. If you find crossed warps, untwine on either or both ends and retwine with the warps in proper order. Continue working from either end.

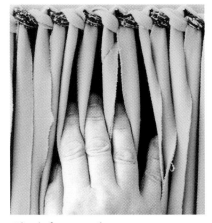

Check for crossed warps.

Complete four rows of checkerboard countered twining. At the end of the fourth row, cut the solid weft and attach a patterned weft strip.

Twine two rows using two patterned wefts. At the end of the second patterned row, cut the weft that's on top of the selvedge, and sew on a solid weft.

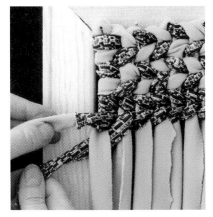

End of the solid strip, with new weft attached.

The sampler's center uses the alternate edge turn for vertical stripes. Twining motions remain the same, and rows should alternate in pitch.

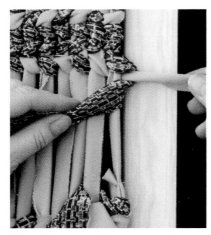

Keep the same color on top at the selvedge.

Complete the turn to line up colors vertically.

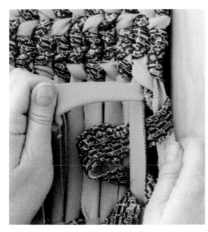

Pull the solid-colored weft until it doesn't show on the side.

End the sampler anywhere in the center section, away from the sides of the frame. Mine required nine rows in the center and a total of 21 rows; yours may need more or fewer. Make adjustments in the center section, keeping the pitch of the last row the opposite of that in the rows above and below.

Sew like colors together to complete the last weft segments, and force the ends vertically through previous rows for at least 1″ to hide them (after you take the sampler off the frame, if you prefer).

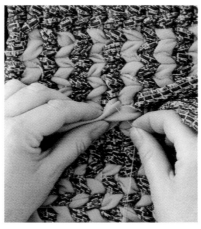

Sew wefts to form the last segments.

Pull weft ends through previous rows to hide them.

Cut off the excess. To reduce bulk, take two weft ends to the back side and hide all of them alongside different warps in both directions.

Carefully remove the sampler from the nails and *immediately* sew the wefts to the warps in the upper left and lower right corners, to keep them from sliding off the selvedges.

Sew the weft to the warp in the corners where the warp starts and ends.

SAME-PITCH TWINING

Repeating the same pitch in several rows makes diagonal patterns. Using the same pitch in taaniko gives a smoother line to an angled pattern. Same-pitch twining can be adapted for three-weft rugs and is normal for curved rugs.

A rectangular rug worked entirely in the same pitch will curl in diagonally opposite corners, which is a safety hazard. Alternating with opposite-pitch sections helps somewhat, but where the pitch direction changes, a rug buckles slightly. Confine same-pitch designs to relatively narrow bands, and use countered twining at the top and bottom to keep the corners flat. Same-pitch twining is not a problem in a curved rug, because the orientation of weft segments changes frequently.

For left-pitch sections in a straight-sided rug, maintain left-pitch twining when twining toward the right. Turn at the right selvedge as if making a regular turn, but cross wefts from bottom to top — *toward the previous row* — to start the next row. This gives left-pitch twining in the rows that work toward the left. Make the regular turn at the left selvedge.

For right-pitch rows worked left to right, cross wefts from bottom to top, working toward the previous row or top of the frame. Use a regular edge turn and work every other row (those headed left) in regular twining. Selvedge turns are similar.

Same-pitch twining; turn at the left selvedge for right-pitch twining (left) and at the right selvedge for left-pitch twining.

Same pitch twining; right-pitch (left) and left-pitch (right).

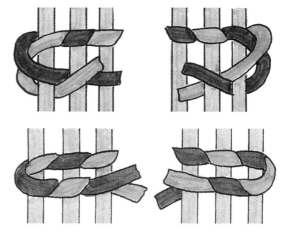

This old Salish rug curls in the corners because of same-pitch twining. It was collected in 1875 by James G. Swan. Catalogue #23427, Department of Anthropology, Smithsonian Institution. Photo by Bobbie Irwin.

Silvia Falett, Ottenbach, Switzerland used same-pitch twining in this small rug to create an interesting pattern. The pitch changes in the middle of each row. Countered twining at the top and bottom help keep corners from curling. Courtesy Silvia Falett.

SAMPLER #2:
Same-Pitch Twining

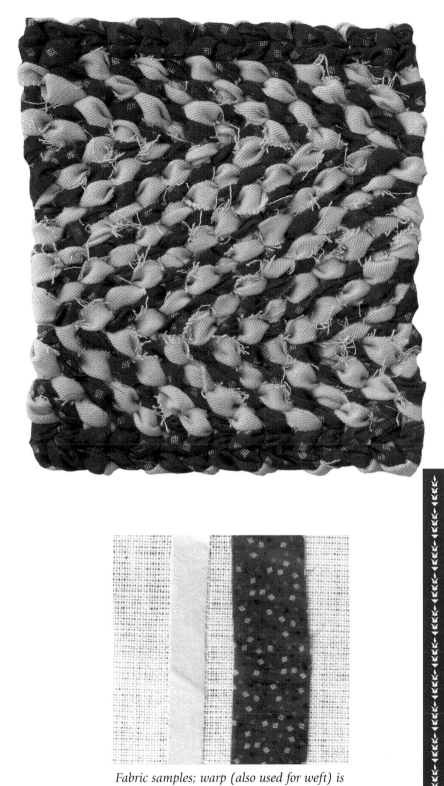

This sampler features diagonal patterns that develop when you repeat rows with the same pitch. The sampler starts and ends with countered twining to keep the corners flat. Where the pitch direction changes, you may notice a slight buckling at the selvedges. Woven fabrics like these, with little stretch, make a firm reversible rug. This sampler uses fabrics of different weights to give you experience balancing weft widths.

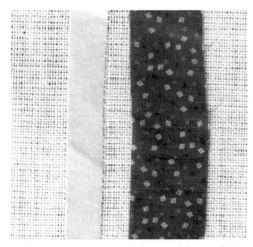

Fabric samples; warp (also used for weft) is at the left.

Frame: Pegged sampler frame.
Warping Method: Continuous.
Warp: Pink denim: 4 yards 1″ wide.
Weft: Lightweight cotton print: 8 yards 2″ wide. Pink denim (same as warp): 7 yards 1″ wide. Choose solid and patterned cotton fabrics of unequal weight, cut to balance.

Warping. Zigzag starting at the upper left, overlapping the end about 3" and pinning it to the first warp temporarily. End in the lower right corner with 15 warps. Pin the end without cutting the excess. Now unpin the start of the warp and sew it to the *second* warp.

Sew the start of the warp to the second warp.

Twining. Start with the print fabric. Fold a weft strip so the ends are uneven, and twine two rows in regular countered twining, starting at the upper left. Enclose the overlapped warp end along with the second warp.

Enclose the overlapped end with the second warp.

Adjust the number of warps or weft widths as needed, then sew the end of the warp to its adjacent warp in the lower right corner and trim off the excess. Complete a row of countered twining on the other end of the frame, using the print weft, and continue from either end.

At the end of the second row, cut the weft which is *underneath* the selvedge and sew a solid strip onto it. Continue in countered twining (left pitch), alternating weft colors.

Sew on solid-colored weft to start the third row.

At the end of the third row, turn by carrying the weft that is on top of the selvedge around first.

Start the turn.

Cross the print weft over the solid *from bottom to top* and place the printed weft under the second warp.

Cross wefts bottom to top.

To complete the next weft segment, cross the solid over the print from bottom to top and under the third warp. Continue across, alternating colors, with a left pitch just as in the row above.

Left-pitch twining, right to left.

Make a regular turn at the left selvedge.

A regular turn.

When twining several rows of the same pitch, every other one is twined in the standard way (twisting toward the untwined warp), and the others will be just the opposite, twisting toward the previous row. Complete four left-pitch rows.

The center section has right-pitch rows. Starting at the left selvedge, cross the wefts bottom-to-top to make right-pitch segments, working toward the previous row and away from the untwined warp.

Rows that work from right to left will be in regular right-pitch twining, with wefts crossing top-to-bottom toward the untwined warp.

Right-pitch twining, right to left.

Work four left-pitch rows on the other end before completing the center section. My sampler has nine rows of right-pitch twining in the center section and 21 total rows; yours may have more or fewer rows, an odd or even number. Make adjustments and finish in the center section. Sew like colors together to complete the final weft segments and hide the wefts.

Slip the sampler off the nails; there is no need to sew the corners. The contrasting warp shows at the top and bottom.

Hide the ends.

Right-pitch twining, left to right.

Sew the last segments.

THREE-WEFT TWINING

This technique creates an interesting color pattern. For variation, use two wefts of the same color or experiment with same-pitch twining. A three-weft rug is reversible; the top side looks like regular twining, but on the back side each weft segment crosses two warps, making the rug extra thick. The side with the shorter weft segments should wear better and be less likely to snag. A three-weft rug is easiest to work in one direction, rather than from both ends.

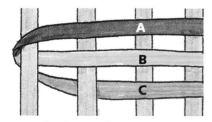

Three-weft color pattern.

Fasten together three wefts of unequal lengths by sandwiching two within the third. Start in the upper left with one weft (A) on top of the selvedge and the other two wefts underneath. Bring the second weft (B) up between the first two warps, and the third weft (C) to the surface between the second and third warps and on top of the third warp. Lay all three strands horizontally, extending to the right.

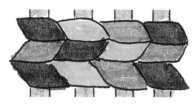

Start the three wefts.

Start twining with A. Cross it over B between the first two warps, top to bottom, take it under the second and third warps, then back to the surface.

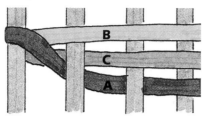

The first twining motion.

Pick up B, cross it over C, and pass it underneath the third and fourth warps, then back to the surface. Repeat, creating left-pitch segments and keeping the colors in the same order. Each weft passes over one warp and under two.

Left-pitch twining with three wefts.

Only two wefts turn around the selvedge. Note which weft is on top of the third warp from the right; this weft will not go around the selvedge. Depending on how many warps you have, this could be any of the three wefts. Put it over the top of the frame, out of the way.

Put the weft on top of the third warp up out of the way between the second and selvedge warps.

With the other two wefts, start a regular turn with the weft that's on top of the selvedge. Take it behind the other weft and under the first *and second* warps, bringing it to the surface between the second and third warps.

Start the turn.

Bring the other weft over the selvedge, under the second and third warps and back to the surface.

Turn the second weft.

Bring the final weft, the one you put up out of the way, around over the second warp and under the next two headed toward the left. This third weft treats the second warp as its selvedge.

Continue twining as before, over one and under two warps, always starting with the weft that's farthest behind.

Rows worked right to left should have a right pitch. Turn at the left side the same way as at the right.

Complete the turn.

Three-Weft Countered Twining

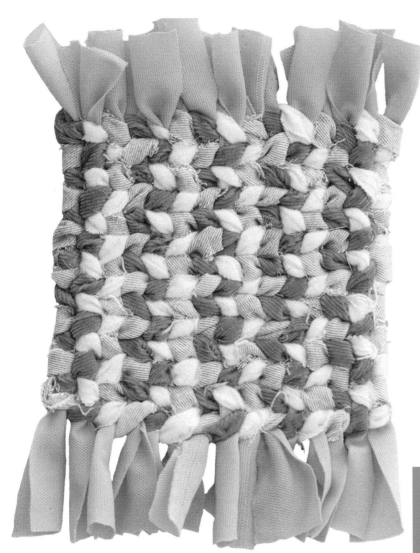

This sampler incorporates fabrics of different weights, textures, and types and built-in fringe from a knit fabric that won't ravel.

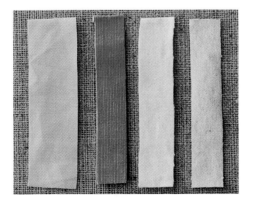

Fabric samples; warp on the left.

Frame: Unpegged sampler frame.

Warping Method: Continuous figure-eight warp wrapped around the ends of the frame.

Warp: Medium-weight knit fabric, 5 yards 2" wide. Choose a color compatible with the wefts.

Weft: 4-1/2 yards each of three heavy woven fabrics in compatible colors: light blue denim and medium-blue corduroy, 1-1/4" wide, and off-white flannel, 1-1/2" wide.

Warping: Loop the end of the warp around the frame, overlapping about 3″ below the top inside of the frame. Pass the warp around the bottom of the frame, back through the center, around the top, through the center, and so forth, following a figure-eight path and ending in the lower right corner with 15 warps.

Figure-eight warping.

Loop the end around the frame and pin; don't cut the excess.

Pin the end without cutting the excess.

Sew the start of the warp to the first warp.

Sew the start to the first warp.

Twining: Sew together unequal lengths of all three wefts. Start twining with dark weft on the selvedge, enclosing the overlapped warp.

First weft segment, enclosing the overlapped warp end with the first warp.

Twine the second segment with white weft and the third with the medium.

Second weft segment.

Third weft segment.

Twine all the way to the right side. The weft that's on top of the second warp from the right will only pass under one warp (the selvedge). With 15 warps, the medium blue will be on top of the right selvedge warp.

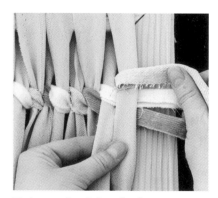

Twine to the right selvedge.

Make any needed changes in weft width or number of warps, remove the pin, and sew the end of the warp.

With 15 warps, the dark blue weft is on top of the third warp from the right and will not go around the selvedge. Take it back and over the top of the frame between the selvedge and adjacent warp, crossing the other wefts from bottom to top.

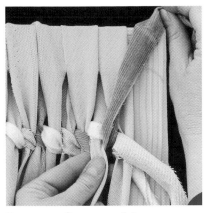

Put one weft up out of the way.

Turn around the selvedge with the other two wefts. The weft that's on top of the selvedge travels behind the other weft and underneath the selvedge to start the second row, coming back to the surface between the second and third warps.

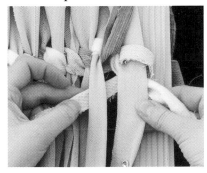

Start the turn.

The weft underneath the selvedge on the first row comes back over the selvedge to start the second row, then under the next two warps before coming back to the surface.

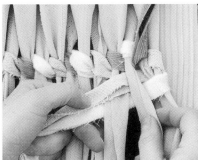

Turn the second weft.

Bring the dark blue weft over the second warp and under the next two warps, heading left.

Complete the turn.

Continue twining with a right pitch.

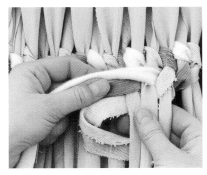

Resume twining.

At the left selvedge, the medium and dark wefts turn around the selvedge, and the white weft stops short, turning around the second warp. No matter how many warps you have, only two wefts turn around each selvedge (always the same two at any one side), but the wefts involved will depend on the number of warps.

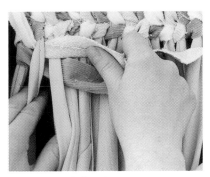

Turn at the left side.

Continue in countered twining until you've covered the stitching at the bottom of the frame.

The end of the sampler.

End at the lower left or right. My sampler has 14 rows; yours may vary, either odd or even.

Remove the sampler from the frame by cutting across the warp at the top and bottom or slip the ends of the frame out to leave loops. Hide the ends alongside the warps on the back side.

Hide the ends.

Stitch all the weft segments to the warps across the top and bottom to keep these rows from slipping.

Stitch the end rows to the warps.

False Tapestry

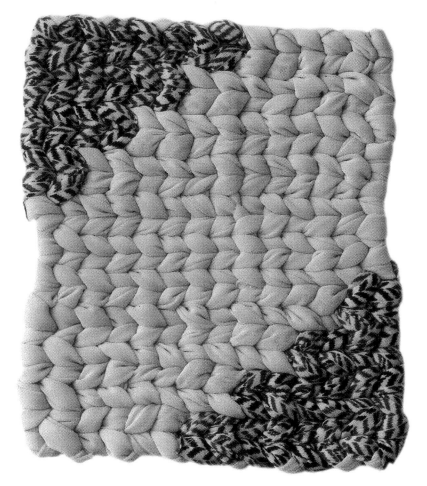

*T*his sampler is a good introduction to graphed designs, using only two colors. Each square of a graph represents one weft segment, and each column is one warp. (The vertical lines in a graph are not warps.) This sampler has an even number of warps. Make adjustments to the number of rows in the center section.

Frame: Pegged sampler frame.

Warping Method: Continuous.

Warp: Lightweight jersey, 4 yards 3″ wide.

Weft: Lightweight jersey: 1 yard patterned fabric 3″ wide; and 4 yards solid (same as warp) 3″ wide.

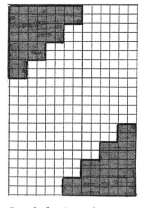

Graph for Sampler #4.

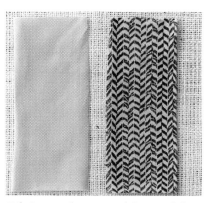

Fabric samples; warp (also used for weft) on the left.

FALSE TAPESTRY

False tapestry creates discontinuous patterns, like tapestry, but it's easier since you just sew on new colors as needed. False tapestry is appropriate for designs with relatively long sections of solid colors and is especially good when there are several colors in a weft row. A good choice for many pictorial rugs, it is one of the best methods for irregular designs, since it allows precise color placement. It is not useful for frequent and intricate color changes. Most false tapestry rugs are reversible, but the top side usually looks better.

Warping: Start at the upper left, ending in the upper right corner with 14 warps. Sew the start of the warp to the second warp. After any needed adjustments, sew the warp end to its adjacent warp and trim the excess.

Sew warp ends to adjacent warps.

Twining: Work the sampler in countered twining. Start at the upper left with two patterned wefts in left-pitch twining until you complete eight weft segments, and cut both wefts between the eighth and ninth warps.

Twine eight segments.

Cut both wefts.

Sew on solid-colored wefts and continue across the first row.

Sew on solid-colored wefts.

Finish the first row.

Start the second row with the solid wefts and right-pitch twining. After twining six segments on the second row, cut off both wefts between the sixth and seventh warps from the right. Sew on patterned wefts, enclosing the patterned wefts inside the solid ones, and

continue across the row. You should have the same number of segments of each color, in the same positions, as for the first row. Repeat the same sequence on the other end of the frame, check for crossed warps, and proceed from either end.

Continue twining, using the graph to tell you where to change colors. The third and fourth rows of the graph show six patterned segments followed by eight solid segments, and the fifth row has four pattern/ten solid. The last row that includes the patterned weft will have very short sections of weft, and you'll have to join on new wefts at the selvedge.

Before you finish the pattern section on one end, complete the equivalent rows on the other end.

The last pattern row.

Finish the sampler near the center, making sure the final row has the opposite pitch from the rows above and below it. My sampler has solid-colored rows in the center, but yours may not have any rows without patterned weft. As long as the patterned sections are identical on both ends, the sampler will look symmetrical. By allowing this kind of leeway in a design, you don't have to twine an exact number of rows to make a pleasing pattern.

TAPESTRY

In twined tapestry, designs are discontinuous and each pattern area has its own two wefts that travel back and forth in their own sections. This sampler introduces both dovetailed and interlocked weft joins. Most tapestry rugs are reversible.

Of the twining techniques included in this book, tapestry may be the most challenging. It works best with fabrics of equal type, weight, and width, especially with the interlocked join. It's particularly important to balance fabrics of different weights.

Tapestry is a good choice for designs with straight sides and regular angles. It's not good for very small pattern areas (blocks), where taaniko excels. Tapestry generally requires fewer stitched joins than false tapestry, so a tapestry rug may be more durable.

For dovetailed tapestry, twine each block in order, right to left when working toward the right, and vice versa. Wherever two blocks meet there is a shared warp, and the warps adjacent to the shared warp are *edge warps*.

With a dovetailed join, one weft from each adjacent block turns around the shared warp. There are several methods, but this one, devised by Lillie Sherwood, best covers the warp on both sides.

Detail of a tapestry rug by Lillie Sherwood.

Note which wefts are on top of the edge warps, adjacent to the shared warp. These will do the joining, going under and then over the shared warp alternately, headed opposite directions. The other wefts stop short of the shared warp and turn around the edge warps, forming larger-than-normal weft segments with exaggerated pitch. The reverse side looks more normal.

Dovetailed tapestry join; only one weft from each block goes around the shared warp.

Weft-interlocked tapestry lacks shared warps between blocks; the edge warps form the block boundaries. The wefts on top of the edge warps join. First, start the other wefts back in opposite directions, turning under and then back over the edge warps. Between the edge warps, cross the right joining weft *over* the left joining weft, then back under the edge warp, working toward the right.

Start of the interlocked tapestry join.

The left joining warp heads left, under its edge warp and over the next.

The completed interlocked join.

In any tapestry join, only one weft from each adjacent block makes the join and the other stops short. Joining all four wefts is too bulky and would distort the warp. When pattern boundaries are vertical, the same two wefts perform the join on successive rows. If the pattern junction is not vertical, the same colors may not always make the join but you always use whichever wefts are on top of the edge warps.

Countered Tapestry Twining

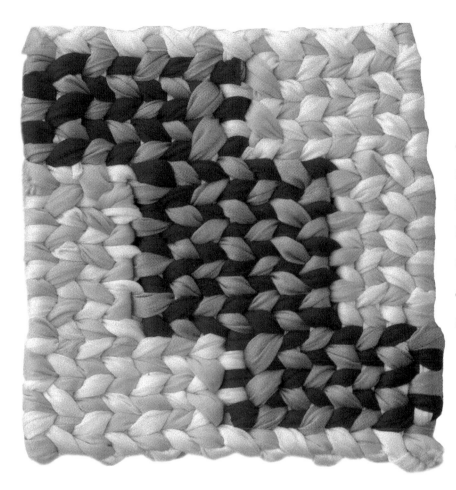

This sampler requires two alternating colors for each pattern area (block), which would be more difficult to accomplish by other methods. To maintain the color alternation, pay close attention to which colors are on top at the start of each block.

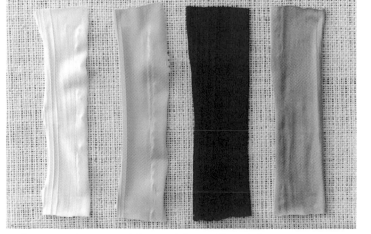

Fabric samples; warp (also used for weft) at left.

Frame: Unpegged sampler frame with suspended wires.
Warping Method: Continuous, in figure-eight fashion.
Warp: Yellow nylon tricot, 3-1/2 yards 2-1/2" wide.
Weft: Nylon tricot 2-1/2" wide; 3 yards of gold, 3-1/2 yards of yellow (same as warp), 3-1/2 yards of red, and 3 yards of orange.

Warping: Lay the frame flat and use twist-ties to position the wires just inside the frame, parallel to the top and bottom and to each other. Pin the warp around the top wire at the upper left. Zigzag the warp around the wires, always front to back, ending in the lower right corner with 15 warps. Pin the end without cutting the excess. Sew the start of the warp to the second warp.

Warp around wires.

Twining: Sew together gold and yellow wefts of unequal length. Start at the upper left with gold on top of the selvedge and twine a row in regular countered twining, with a left pitch.

Start the first row.

Make the regular (checkerboard) turn and start the second row. Adjust fabric widths as needed, but don't add or subtract warps; sew the end of the warp to the adjacent warp, and trim excess.

Rotate the frame and twine a row on the opposite end, using the same colors and starting with the gold weft on top of the selvedge. Check for crossed warps and make any needed corrections. Continue working from either end.

Check for crossed warps.

The first tapestry section starts on the second row, since it's easier to work tapestry after the warps are aligned by a row of twining. The two blocks have their own wefts that go back and forth only within their pattern areas. This section uses a dovetailed weft join. The center (eighth) warp is the shared warp; one weft from each pattern block wraps around the shared warp.

Continuing with yellow and gold wefts, twine right to left across seven warps, stopping short of the shared warp. Sew together red and orange wefts and twine toward the left, starting with the red weft on top of the shared warp.

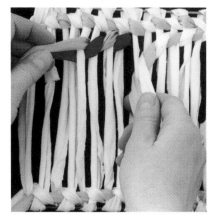

Start the first pattern blocks.

All segments in this row have a right pitch. Make a normal turn at the left selvedge and start the third row with the red and orange wefts.

Before you reach the shared warp, start the yellow and gold wefts back toward the right. Note which weft (yellow) is on top of the seventh warp, adjacent to the shared warp. This is the weft that will wrap around the shared warp on each row. Take the yellow weft under the shared warp, then back over it and under the adjacent warp, treating the shared warp like a selvedge.

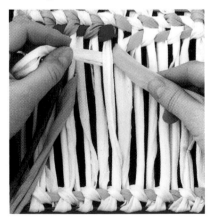

Start the dovetailed join around the shared warp.

Cross the gold weft over the yellow, top to bottom, between the shared and adjacent warps. The gold weft goes over the adjacent warp and under the next warp below the yellow weft. Continue twining toward the right.

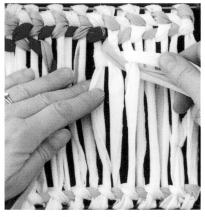

Complete the turn for the right block.

Twine the red and orange wefts across to finish the second row. The orange weft is underneath the warp adjacent to the shared warp and is the one that will stop short. The red weft, which is over the adjacent warp, wraps around the shared warp to make the join (under, then over).

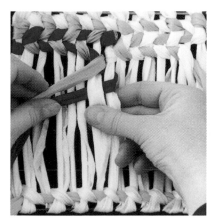

Dovetail with the left block.

The orange weft crosses over the red weft between the shared and adjacent warps, stays on top of the adjacent warp, and under the next warp.

Complete five rows in countered twining with the dovetailed join, always using the same shared warp and the same wefts around it, in the same order. One pattern block starts a new row before the other wefts finish the previous row, but both pattern areas must end up with the same number of rows, with the same pitch across each row.

At the end of the fifth pattern row (sixth row from the top), sew together the yellow and gold wefts at the center, and hide the ends as if you were finishing the sampler. Hide the red and orange wefts and cut them or sew a gold weft onto the red one and a yellow weft to the orange one. Rotate the frame and repeat the five pattern rows at the other end, using new wefts in the same color sequence.

The center of the sampler has three pattern blocks and uses an interlocked weft join. There are no shared warps; the wefts join between warps. The same colors do the joining on each row. However, different weft colors interlock at the left and right sides of the central block.

Start the center section with three sets of wefts, two pairs of yellow and gold and one pair of orange and red. The gold-and-yellow block on the right starts on the fourth weft from

the right, with yellow on top. The center block, red and orange, starts with red on top of the fifth warp from the left. The left-hand block starts with gold on top of the left selvedge. Don't interlock them until you start the second row.

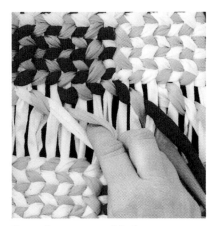

Start three pattern blocks.

Start the next row with the right-hand block. The join will occur between the fourth and fifth warps from the right. Note which wefts are on top of these warps; at the right, gold, and at the left, the red is on top on the first row. The other wefts — orange and yellow — do not make the join. Take both of them under, then over the edge warps headed opposite directions. The yellow starts the third row while the orange is still on the second row. Now pick up the other wefts. Cross the gold (right-hand) weft over the red (left-hand) weft, then back under it and under the fourth warp, headed toward the right.

Start the interlocked join.

Take the red weft under the fifth warp, headed left.

Complete the join.

Continue twining toward the left with the center wefts. This block will join the left-hand pattern block between the fourth and fifth warps from the left. Again, the wefts that are underneath these warps — red and gold — will stop short and do not interlock. The other wefts — yellow and orange — make the join and then head opposite directions.

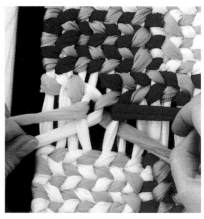

Interlock the left and middle blocks.

Complete the center section in countered twining, and finish the sampler at the bottom of this section, making sure that the pitch of the final row is the opposite of the rows above and below. My sampler required nine rows in the center section and 21 total rows; yours may vary, but it will be an odd number. Make any adjustments in the center section.

You will end up with six weft ends on the last row, two at one selvedge and four at the two pattern-block junctions. Remove the twist-ties and pull out the wires.

Sew weft pairs together to form the last segments, and hide the ends as usual.

Ending the sampler.

Taaniko

Taaniko (pronounced tar-nee-kor) is the Maori word for the technique they perfected, which has appeared independently in other cultures. Rugs from the Pacific Northwest incorporate taaniko twining for intricate patterning. Taaniko is the best method for intricate pattern detail, especially with three or fewer colors in any row. It takes more fabric than regular twining, and it creates a thicker, nonreversible rug. The right side of taaniko resembles regular twining. The back side has horizontal ribs. The dominant weft requires considerably more fabric than other wefts, and since it stays on the surface most of the time, you can use up to four-yard strips of the dominant weft.

Taaniko with two colors carries both wefts throughout a row, but one remains hidden except where you want it to appear. In a finished project, the hidden weft follows a straight path across the back side, while the dominant weft makes a full twist between warps to stay on the surface.

Taaniko twining.

Traditionally, though, the Maori twine with the hidden weft. Keep the dominant weft on the surface. Bring the hidden weft over it, top to bottom, *between warps*, without crossing a warp. Take the hidden weft to the back side again and pull gently until it no longer shows on the surface.

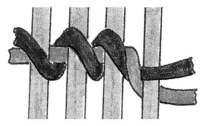

The "hidden" weft (turquoise here) crosses top to bottom over the surface weft without crossing any warp; pull it until only the surface weft shows.

To make the other weft appear, make one weft segment in regular twining, exchanging weft positions. Then the former surface weft wraps around the other. A single weft segment of a color can show on the surface any place you want.

Change surface colors.

Selvedge turns are similar to the turn for vertical columns in regular twining. Where you want the same color on top of the selvedge for successive rows, bring the hidden weft over the surface weft, top to bottom, outside the selvedge. Keep the surface weft on top of the selvedge to start the next row.

Turn at the selvedge.

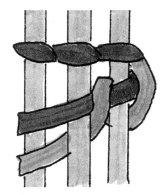

Start the next row.

Pull the hidden weft until it disappears.

SAMPLER #6:
Countered Taaniko

Although only part of this sampler is patterned, the entire sampler is worked in taaniko, carrying both colors throughout. The design is flexible so you can add or subtract rows at the center.

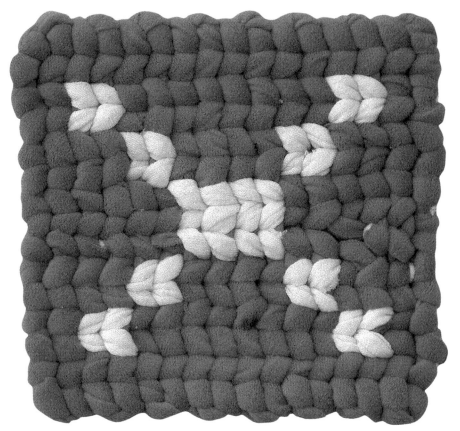

Frame: Unpegged sampler frame with suspended wires.
Warping Method: Warp loops.
Warp: Blue velour, 2-1/3 yards 1-3/4″ wide.
Weft: Blue velour, same as warp, for the dominant (background) color, 9 yards 1-3/4″ wide. White knit jersey for the pattern, 4-1/3 yards 1-3/4″ wide.

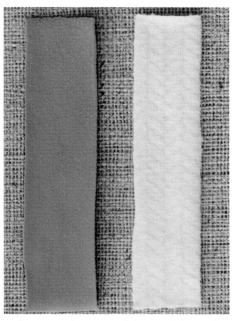

Fabric samples; warp (also used for weft) on left.

Warping: Cut eight strips, each 14-3/4″ long (or twice the warp length plus the width). Sew each strip into a loop.

Make a warp loop.

Place loops side by side on the wires, using twist-ties to tension the wires and keep them parallel to the ends of the frame.

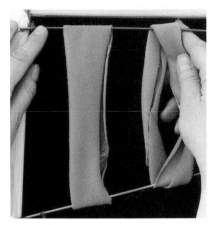

Put warp loops on wires.

Twining: Sew together one weft of each color; the background (blue) weft should be longer. Twine both strands of each warp loop before going on to the next.

First and second warps are part of the same loop.

With blue on top of the first weft, start in the upper left corner and twine with blue on the surface for the first two rows. Wrap the hidden weft (white) over the blue, top to bottom between warps.

Cross the light weft over the surface weft between warps, top to bottom.

Take the white to the back side, and pull.

Take the light weft to the back side and pull gently until it disappears.

To turn at the selvedge, wrap the white over the blue, keep blue on top to start the second row, and pull the white until it disappears on the edge.

Turn at the right.

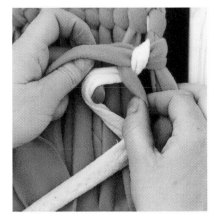

Pull the light weft until it disappears at the side.

Continue twining as before.

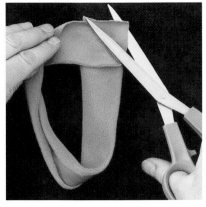

Resume twining with the light weft.

The pattern is designed for 16 warps, so change weft width to make any adjustments. After twining one or two rows on the top, rotate the frame and twine at least one row on the other end, keeping the warps in order.

Work from either end, following the graph. Each square on the graph represents one weft segment. The pattern starts on the third row from the top, on the third warp.

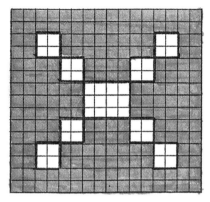

Graph for taaniko sampler.

To bring the white weft to the surface, interchange weft positions exactly as in regular twining.

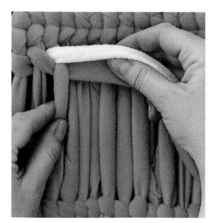

Bring the light weft to the surface with regular twining.

Keep the white weft on the surface to form two weft segments, wrapping the blue weft around the white weft between the warps and pulling the blue to hide it.

Wrap with the dark weft.

After two white segments, use regular twining to bring the blue weft back to the surface and the white to the back side for eight segments, maintaining left pitch.

Twine eight segments with dark weft on top before bringing the light weft back to the surface.

After four pattern rows, rotate the frame and repeat. Finish this sampler in the blue area of the center section. My sampler has three rows in the center; yours may have more or fewer (an odd number). To make an even number of rows in the center, you would have to start the opposite end of the sampler from right to left with right pitch.

End with blue (background) wefts on the surface and the white wefts on the back side. Hide the ends vertically alongside the warps on the front side, as usual. On the back side, hide the wefts horizontally instead of vertically.

Remove the wires; no other finishing is needed.

SALISH-STYLE TWINING

Salish patterns are geometric, primarily diamonds, zigzags, triangles, and stepped patterns, with some stylized animal motifs. Most rectangular Salish rugs were made on upright looms. Regular two-weft twining creates familiar checkerboard and columnar patterns. Intricate patterning is worked in taaniko, and angular designs in tapestry.

Salish-style tapestry is suitable for angular or irregular patterns; you can work part of a motif before filling in the background. First work areas that are decreasing in size, whether they are pattern or background.

To work this tapestry pattern in sections rather than one line at a time, first twine the upper blue triangles, then the white area around them. At the halfway point, start twining the white areas first and finish with the lower blue triangles.

If the angle is constant and wefts don't always meet on the same warp (as they do for vertical lines), you needn't join wefts from adjoining blocks — this is called *slit* tapestry.

Warp and weft spacing determines how steep an angle you can twine; with the same number of warps and weft rows per inch, you can make 45-degree angles; otherwise, a graphed pattern will appear distorted in the finished piece (compressed or elongated compared to the original graph). A stair-stepped pattern on graph paper will have angled sides that appear smoother in the actual rug. To center a diamond or other pattern, you may need an odd number of warps. Calculate the total number you will need before you start working. With some angled patterns, it's okay if the background and pattern don't have the same number of rows.

Most Salish rugs have same-pitch twining, which curls the corners. For safety's sake, use countered twining.

At the point of a diamond or triangle, wrap the wefts entirely around the center warp for the first row.

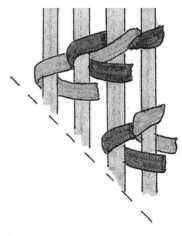

Start at a point.

As you work an angle away from a point, take the weft that's on top of the warp next to the pattern boundary back under that same warp, headed the other direction, to start the next row. The second weft goes over, then under the warp that forms the pattern boundary.

Slit tapestry on an angle.

Pattern and background wefts do not travel around the same warps on the same rows. This leaves some warp exposed on the reverse side of the rug; dovetail or interlock wefts for a reversible rug.

SAMPLER #7:
Salish-Style Twining

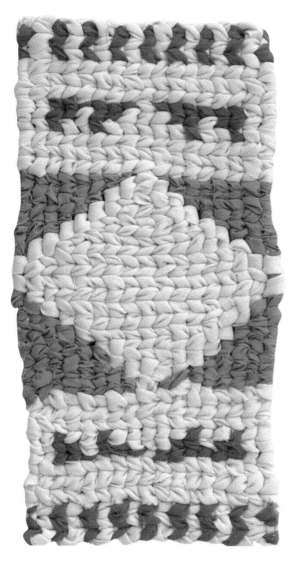

*I*n keeping with Salish tradition, I've used a Salish-style loom and narrower warp and weft strips than I often use. This sampler in countered twining incorporates typical Salish patterns.

This project requires careful attention to center patterns symmetrically, lengthwise, and crosswise. Depending on how many weft rows you have per inch, the (imaginary) side points of the diamond may extend beyond the sides, as mine do, or you may end up with background weft completely surrounding the diamond. Twine to the base of the diamond before starting the other end, to determine the pitch to use for starting the opposite end.

Frame: Salish sampler frame.
Warping Method: Reverse warping.
Warp: Medium-weight knit fabric, off-white, 8 yards 1″ wide.
Weft: Off-white knit, same as the warp, 17 yards 1″ wide; rose cotton broadcloth, 5 yards 1-1/2″ wide; blue cotton batiste, 6-1/2 yards 1-1/2″ wide.

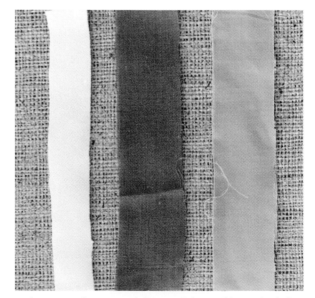

Fabric samples; warp (also used for weft) on the left.

Warping: Use twist-ties to suspend the wire parallel to the top dowel and a few inches below it. Tape the ends of the wire to keep the warps from slipping off and protect you from scratches. Loop the warp around the wire at the left side and pin it in place temporarily.

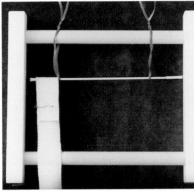

Loop the warp around the wire.

Carry the warp down around the lower dowel, front to back, up the back side, over the top dowel (back to front), and then around the wire adjacent to the start of the warp. Reverse directions, taking the warp strand back over the top, down the back, up the front from the bottom, and around the wire again. Each time the warp meets the wire, it loops around the wire and reverses direction.

The warp reverses direction each time it goes around the wire.

Each trip around the frame creates a single warp, half on the front side and half on the back. At least at the start, wind the warp loosely so the wire stays parallel to the dowel and perpendicular to the sides. After you've warped half the wire, pull on the warps to even the tension, but don't make them too tight. You must be able to fit your index fingers between the warp and the dowels. Remove the twist-ties before twining.

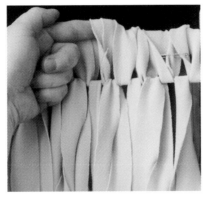

The warp must be loose enough so you can fit your fingers between the warp and the dowels.

Wind on 17 warps (count only below the wire) and loop the warp around the wire at the right side. Push the warps tightly together to fit them on.

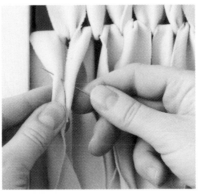

End the warp at the upper right; sew the start to the second warp on the front side.

Pin the end temporarily without trimming off the excess. Sew the start of the warp to the second warp. Check to make sure no warps cross through the center.

Twining: With off-white and rose wefts, start at the left side below the wire in regular left-pitch twining.

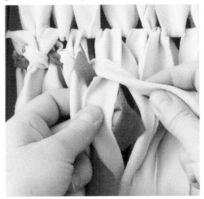

Regular twining.

Twine only the top layer of the warps; don't pick up any from the back side or above the wire. After the first row, adjust the weft width and warp numbers as needed, maintaining an odd number, and sew the end of the warp to the adjacent warp above the wire. Snug the row up against the wire by pulling warp *pairs*. Do not start working from the other end yet.

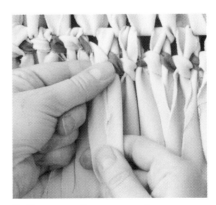

Pull warp pairs to move the row up to the wire.

Move the wire, with the warp on it, to the top of the upper dowel, keeping them parallel. Mark the halfway point on the warp at the bottom of the lower dowel. The marks help you keep the pattern symmetrical.

Mark the halfway point.

Move the wire and warp down again on the front side, to a comfortable position. Work the first three rows in a columnar pattern by keeping the same color on top at the selvedge turns.

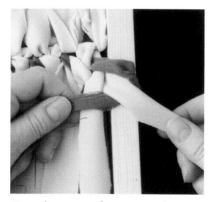

Keep the rose weft on top at the turn.

At the end of the third row, cut the rose weft and attach an off-white weft. Work the next three rows with two off-white wefts and the regular edge turn. As you work, use both hands to gently rotate the entire sampler and wire up and around the top dowel.

At the start of the seventh row, attach a rose-colored weft and continue with one off-white weft. Work the next three rows in taaniko, following the graph: with 17 warps, the first row has two off-white, six rose, one off-white, six rose, and two off-white. Work three more rows in regular twining with two off-white wefts; attach blue wefts at the selvedge.

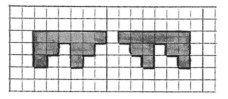

Graph for the taaniko section.

Mark the center warp with a safety pin, some distance below the previous weft row.

Mark the center warp.

Because the background decreases as the diamond gets wider, work the background first. Each blue area has its separate pair of wefts, and the off-white diamond has its own.

If you have 17 warps, twine across eight of them with the blue wefts and leave the center (marked) warp untwined. Start the other blue area with eight weft segments. Each background row should have the same pitch on each side.

Start the blue background; each side has separate wefts.

Blue wefts decrease by one warp each row, leaving an untwined diamond in the center.

Each background block decreases one warp each row.

Start the diamond with the off-white wefts around the middle warp and increase in both directions as you fill in the diamond.

Start the diamond.

The diamond increases as the background decreases.

Remove the pin. The halfway mark on the warps is the horizontal center of the diamond. In my sampler, the off-white diamond extends to the selvedges, so the background is not continuous. Because I needed to resume using the blue background wefts within two rows, I held these wefts parallel to the selvedge warps and twined around the warps and the blue wefts together until I was ready to start the background again. This is easier and more secure than cutting the wefts.

Carry the background wefts down the selvedge.

When you get halfway, reverse the angles so the bottom of the diamond decreases as the background areas increase. Work the second half of the diamond before you work the background.

Complete the diamond, then the background.

Finish the diamond and one more row before starting at the other end of the warp.

Work one row below the diamond to determine which side to start the other end from.

In my sampler this row has right pitch, but yours might be left. Since the bottom section has an even number of rows, same as the top, the pitch and working direction of this row will be the *opposite* of the row next to the wire.

Start twining from the other end with the wire in a comfortable position, using the same colors and patterns and pink on top of the selvedge, and enclosing warps in the proper order.

Start the other end.

Here I worked left to right; you might need to start right to left (see above). Finish in the solid off-white area near the central diamond. Remove the sampler by pulling out the wire before hiding weft ends as usual.

Remove the sampler by pulling out the wire.

CIRCULAR TWINING

In circular rugs, as in basketry, twining starts at the center of radiating warps and spirals outward. As the diameter increases, you must add warps to keep the weft segments approximately the same size and the rug flat; add new warps with each 1″ to 2″ increase in radius. Because the warps are farther apart with each row and you don't add new warps on each row, you must twine more loosely as the distance between warps increases. When using taaniko, cross wefts towards the outside and avoid pulling too tightly.

Taaniko for circular twining.

Some people twine circular rugs on hoops that hold the warp taut. However, it's easy to twine on a table without any support for the warps, which lets you manipulate both warps and wefts as needed. It's not necessary to change the pitch direction. The constantly changing angle of the weft segments prevents the curling you get in a same-pitch rectangular rug.

Choose left- or right-pitch twining, clockwise or counter-

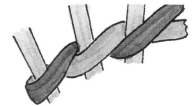

Right-pitch, clockwise twining.

clockwise — whatever feels most natural or best suits your design.

Left-pitch, counterclockwise twining.

Cross wefts toward the outside of the rug (away from the center). Mark the first warp with a safety pin and always start a new color or pattern on the first warp.

A large rug requires many warps, and it's too bulky to include them all at the start. Begin with at least four strands but no more than eight, crossed at their centers (half of each strand, the radius, is one warp). As rug size increases, add new warp pairs at regular intervals to maintain approximately the same spacing. New warps do not cross the center. Fold a new warp strand in half and tie it at the fold to the previous weft row temporarily. After twining the new warps in place, remove the tie.

Some pattern effects (such as spiraling colors) require an odd number of warps. Anchor a single new warp into a few completed weft rows, in the same way you hide wefts when finishing a rug, or cut a strip half the normal width and treat the doubled strand as a single warp.

Each warp should be at least 4″ longer than the planned radius. New warps should be at least as long as other exposed warps. Lengthen warps by attaching new strands. While it's

best to add new warps at regular intervals, you may delay adding warps for a round or two to avoid disrupting a pattern. Whenever possible, add warps on solid-colored rows.

If your warp color is different from the first weft color(s), and you don't want the warp to show at the center, tack a small piece of the weft to the overlapped warp strands at the center before you start. Do the same on the back side if you want both sides the same. A circular rug without taaniko is reversible.

Start with one weft on top of the first two warps and the other weft beneath them, then bring the second weft back to the surface.

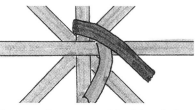

Start at the center with right pitch, clockwise.

For the first round, enclose two warps at a time, then switch to twining around single warps for subsequent rows. Bring the weft that starts under the warps toward the center. The weft on top of warps one and two crosses over the other between warps two and three, away from the center.

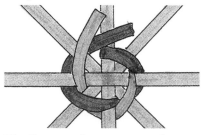

The first round: over two, under two.

Sampler #8:
Circular Twining

A small sampler like this one progresses quickly, but as the diameter increases, so do the number of warps and the time it takes to complete a round. Part way through this sampler, I've added a single warp to make the pattern spiral instead of radiate, creating the illusion of motion. To avoid interrupting the spiral, don't add warps in that pattern area. I worked this sampler counterclockwise; you'd get similar results working clockwise.

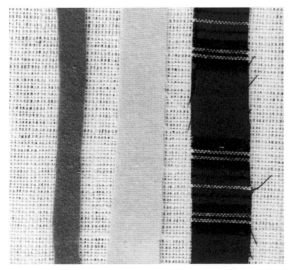

Fabric samples; warp (also used for weft) on the left.

Frame: None; hoop optional.
Warping Method: Radial.
Warp: Medium-weight wool, medium blue, 3/4" wide x 14" long, 7 yards total (each strand is two warps).
Weft: Medium-weight blue wool, same as the warp, 3 yards 3/4" wide; lightweight wool, light blue, 7 yards 1-1/4" wide; lightweight wool, red plaid, 3 yards 1-1/4" wide.

Warping: Cross four warp strands at their centers, radiating evenly to form eight warps. Tack them together to prevent shifting (optional).

Radiating warps.

To hide the warp (which is different from the first wefts), sew on a short piece of the weft fabric at the center (optional).

Twining: Pick one warp as the first warp and mark its end with a safety pin until you finish the sampler. With two light blue wefts, twine counterclockwise, enclosing two warps at a time for the first round only. Pull snugly and even out the warps if you haven't tacked them together.

Twine the first round counter-clockwise.

For subsequent rows, twine around one warp at a time,

crossing wefts in an outward direction. After three rounds, add a pair of warps after each two original warps (four new pairs, 16 total warps), holding them in place temporarily with twist-ties around the previous weft row.

Add a warp pair after each two original warps.

Twine one more round with light blue wefts. Attach two red wefts and twine one round, starting on the first warp. At the end of the round, attach a single warp at any point by pulling it through previous rows.

Attach a single warp at the end of the red round.

Twine three rows without adding warps, alternating red and light blue. Resume twining at the first warp with two light blue wefts. On this row, add nine new pairs of warps, evenly

distributed, for a total of 35. Because the rest of the sampler is unpatterned, it's not necessary to return to an even number of warps.

Attach new warps.

Twine two rows of light blue, then one row with two medium blue wefts. End on the last warp, sew wefts together, and pull weft and warp ends in alongside adjacent warps to secure them, on the back side of the sampler.

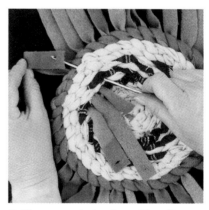

Pull warp ends in alongside adjacent warps.

You can work clockwise or counterclockwise; I prefer the opposite direction from the way I twined. To reduce bulk, stagger the ends by pulling some through three rows and some through four. Trim off the excess.

OVAL TWINING

Like circular twined rag rugs, oval (elliptical) rugs are made from the centers outward, like baskets. An oval rug starts with parallel warps, however, and warps radiate only at the curved sides. Cut the parallel warp strands at least 8" longer than the shortest planned dimension of the rug. Each strand serves as two warps.

Twine the first two or more rows at the center back and forth, as for a rectangular rug, with same-pitch or countered twining. If working without a hoop, you may tape or pin down one end of the warps to start, remembering they will pull together as you twine. After you add side warps, work the rest of an oval rug in spiral fashion, using same-pitch twining (right or left pitch, clockwise or counterclockwise).

The length and depth of the center determine the overall shape. If the center rows are wide and relatively few in number, the finished rug will be a wide oval. A finished rug will lie flatter with only two or three central rows.

An oval rug is easier than a circular one, because you only add warps at the sides. The number of warps in the center stays relatively constant, so confine detailed patterning to these areas. Keep original strands as parallel as possible, maintaining the same spacing.

A continuous pattern that makes a complete circuit may require a specific multiple of warps; restrict it to a narrow band without adding new warps. Graph a pattern first, to know how many warps to start with.

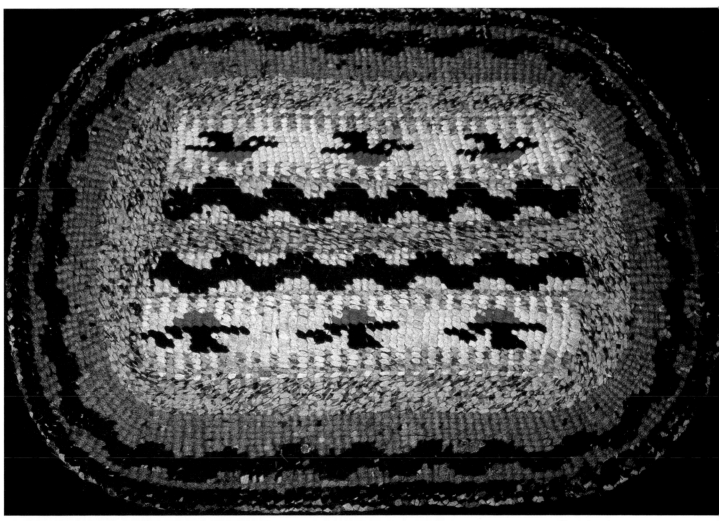

This Nuu-chah-nulth rug from British Columbia has an unusually large rectangular center. Mary McNeill Sieburth Collection, Catalogue #18706, Royal British Columbia Museum.

SAMPLER #9:
Oval Twining

I worked this sampler clockwise in right-pitch twining. The opposite direction gives similar results. The central section is long and narrow, like the finished sampler. The green pattern band, worked in taaniko, continues all the way around the sampler and requires a specific multiple of warps. The pattern becomes distorted on the sides, where the warps radiate.

Frame: None; hoop optional.

Warping Method: Individual warps, radiating at the sides.

Warp: Medium-weight knit fabric, medium rust, 1-1/4″ wide x 13″ long, 8-1/2 yards total (each strand is two warps).

Weft: Heavy woven cotton, light rust, 10 yards 1″ wide; suede-like woven fabric, dark rust, 1-1/4 yards 1″ wide; medium-weight wool, dark green, 3 yards 1″ wide; medium-weight knit, same as the warp, 3-3/4 yards 1-1/4″

Fabric samples; warp (also used for weft) is at left.

Warping: Lay 12 warp strands alongside each other. Mark the first warp on the left with a safety pin and start new colors and patterns on the first warp.

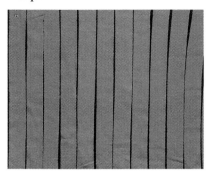

Start with parallel warps.

Twining: Starting on the marked warp, at about the center of the strands, twine left to right with right-pitch twining, using light rust for both wefts.

Right-pitch twining.

Continue in right-pitch twining, working the second row right to left.

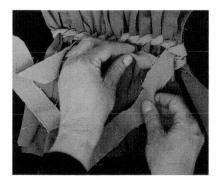

Start the second row.

Adjust the warps to center the first rows of weft.

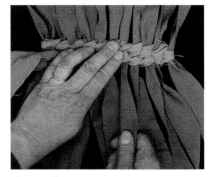

Center the warps.

As you approach the first warp at the end of the second row, add a pair of warps on the left side (one strand folded at its center) and twine around them.

Add two warps.

Work in spiral fashion for each successive round, clockwise.

Add another pair of warps (28 total) on the right side as you work the first round with light rust.

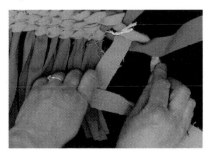

Add warps on the right.

Continue to add warps as needed on both sides, on the same rounds. After one circuit with light rust, twine one round with two dark rust wefts and one round with light rust, adding two more pairs of warps (32 total) on this last round. Do not add any warps for the next three rounds.

Start the taaniko patterning with green and light rust wefts.

Start the taaniko pattern.

Starting with green on top of the first warp, working in taaniko and wrapping the hidden weft around the other from the center outwards, twine one green, one rust, three green, one rust, three green, etc., following the bottom line of the graph, all the way around.

The pattern requires a multiple of four warps, since the *pattern repeat* is four warps wide. A pattern repeat is the smallest number of segments (graph squares) that will reproduce a pattern when it is repeated; no matter where you start in the design, the pattern repeat is the same number.

Continue with green and light rust wefts for the next round, alternating colors on the surface in regular twining (one green, one rust, etc.), following the middle line of the graph.

Regular twining for the middle row.

Use taaniko for the third pattern round (top of graph).

Taaniko for the top row.

Add two pairs of warps (40 total) on each side as you work the next row, using two light rust wefts. Use two medium-rust wefts for the last round.

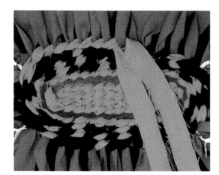

Add warps.

End on the last warp, sew wefts together to form the last weft segment and hide weft and warp ends alongside adjacent warps on the back side.

Sew the last segment.

Graph for taaniko section; the colored part is one pattern repeat.

CARING FOR TWINED RAG RUGS

Frequent machine-washing is hard on any textile, and I don't recommend it for twined rugs. A wet warp is difficult to dry, especially in a humid climate, and it can rot or mildew. The heat and tumbling action of an automatic dryer also stress a rug. Dry cleaning uses wet chemicals that can also soak a warp, and it's expensive and impractical for rag rugs.

If you plan to wash a rug or will use it where it is exposed to moisture frequently (in a bathroom or mud room), use a string warp or plastic clothesline that will dry quickly and resist rot.

Stain resistors and stain removers are chemicals that may shorten the life of a rug. On the other hand, dirt and grit cut into textiles, so some cleaning is necessary. Regular vacuuming and surface cleaning will keep your rug in good condition for many years. Use a scrub brush and suds to keep a rug bright, taking care not to soak the rug all the way through. Avoid shaking or beating a rug.

A time-honored technique for cleaning rag rugs, if you live where it snows in the winter, is to lay the rug flat on clean, dry snow and gently work snow into it on both sides. Brush off the snow before it melts.

Constant exposure to bright sunlight weakens and fades most fabrics. Linen and some synthetics are relatively resistant to fading and light damage.

Chapter 4

Projects

These rugs use many equipment, warping, and pattern variations. Refer to the samplers in Chapter 3 for detailed instructions. Yardages are the approximate combined lengths of the strips, not the uncut fabric. Even with identical fabrics, your yardage, strip width, and spacing might vary, so be sure to sample and allow extra fabric. The finished dimensions given may vary slightly from the original set-up.

For similar results, substitute comparable fabrics and colors. Or improvise using these designs as inspiration, with your choice of fabrics, colors, and equipment. Cut different fabrics to balance, in the direction of least stretch. Sample a few rows before cutting your entire fabric supply, especially when precise pattern alignment is required, and read all the instructions for a project before you start. Time estimates include fabric preparation, warping, twining, and finishing.

*T*he turquoise fabric shines like its namesake gem against the darker background of this three-weft rug. The light-colored backing of the quilted knit fabric shows through along the quilting lines, like the veins in true turquoise.

I twined this rug on a floor loom, but you can use any type of frame. Although I rarely use a nonfabric warp, three-weft twining creates extra bulk, so the yarn I used for warp worked quite well. With either a yarn or fabric warp, you can use the warp as fringe or make four finished edges. Since three-weft twining works best from one direction, it's easier not to have to twine the last row right up against wire or pegs; you can always weave in the extra warp if you desire an unfringed rug.

Rectangular Rug: 23-1/2" x 38"

Estimated Time: 20 hours

Technique: Countered three-weft twining

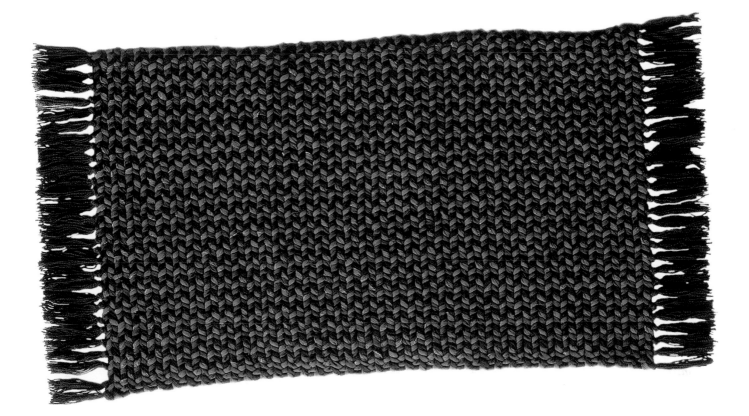

Frame: Floor loom or any frame of adequate length

Warp: For each warp, I used four strands of wool yarn (approximately 1440 yards per pound), 2 yards long, 480 yards total (6-1/2 ounces). I added leftover warp to the fringe. You could use fewer strands of a heavier yarn. If you prefer a fabric warp, choose one of the darker fabrics. For an unfringed rug on a frame, make each warp 40" long.

Warping Method: On a frame, use any preferred method. For a standard loom, wind the warp with one cross as for normal weaving. Remove heddle frames, move the heddles out of the way, or distribute heddles evenly between the warp strands. A coarse reed is optional to keep warps aligned.

Warps Per Inch: 2-1/2

Number of Warps: 60 groups of four, two groups per dent in a five-dent reed. If you use a different spacing, you'll need a different number of warps (e.g. 48 warps at two warps per inch). Treat multiple strands as single warps.

Weft: Three knit fabrics of medium weight, approximately 70 yards of each, 1-1/4" wide. The dark navy blue looks black in the rug. The intermediate color is dark marine blue, and the bright turquoise is a quilted knit with interlocking layers.

Weft Rows Per Inch: 2

Number of Weft Rows: 72 (can be odd or even)

Fabric samples; warp yarn at left.

Instructions

Fasten together one weft of each color, lengths staggered. Start with the darkest fabric on top of the first warp and under the next two warps; the medium color under the selvedge, on top of the second warp, and under the next two; and the lightest color under the first two warps and on top of the third.

If you plan to leave some warp as fringe or weave in the ends later, leave at least 8" extra warp at the start and end of the rug. Twining on a loom is like working from the bottom of a frame up, so the motions are the reverse of normal. The twining motion is away from you, toward the untwined warp. I started at the right side and worked toward the left for the first row, with left-pitch twining. On a frame, work from the top downward in the normal fashion.

Make the normal three-weft turn. On a loom with 60 warps, light and medium wefts turn around the left selvedge, and the dark weft turns around the second warp. At the right side, dark and light wefts turn around the selvedge, and the medium-color weft turns around the second warp. Working top down on a frame, these combinations are reversed.

The first two rows establish the offset color pattern for the whole rug. No colors should line up horizontally or vertically; if they do, untwine and make a correction where the pattern changes.

Twine the entire rug in one direction and finish the warp ends as desired. To make fuller fringe, tie on 16" sections of yarn, four strands at a time. I used what was left on the loom. Tie adjacent warps (four strands each) in a loose half knot, then loop the supplemental yarn through from the front with a loose lark's-head knot.

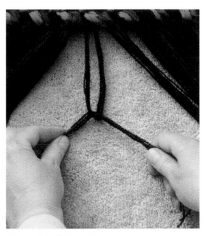

Start the fringe knot.

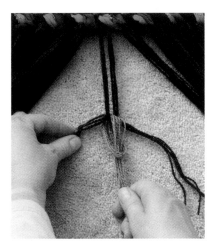

Tie on extra fringe (light-colored yarn used for photo contrast).

Pull on the original warps to snug the knots up against the edge of the rug.

Bring knots to the edge.

Tighten the knots.

Tighten the knot.

Tie an overhand knot with the entire group. Trim the fringe to 4".

Overhand knot.

If you don't want to add more yarn for the fringe, tie adjacent warp groups together to keep the wefts from slipping off. If you don't want fringe, hide warp ends alongside adjacent warps or bind the edges.

BAREFOOT DELIGHT

Bath Mat:
24″ x 15-1/2″

Estimated Time:
6-1/2 hours

Technique:
Regular countered twining with edge-turn variations

*T*his rug combines factors I usually avoid, yet it functions exactly as intended. I used a pegged frame, nonfabric warp, bulky and ravelly wefts, light colors, and loose twining to make a rug designed to absorb moisture. You don't always have to follow the rules for successful results! With the relatively wide warp and weft spacing, Barefoot Delight works up quickly.

I designed this rug as a soft, flexible, and absorbent bath mat. I chose textured fabrics and a warp that would not mildew or rot, and I twined loosely for a soft, spongy texture. This rug isn't appropriate for your mud room, but it will pamper your bare toes!

Frame: Pegged frame, 26″ wide x 18″ long, constructed of canvas stretchers with 23 finishing nails spaced 1″ apart along each 26″ section. Align the first nail on the bottom section midway between the first two nails on the top section (inset 1/2″).

Warp: Plastic clothesline, 20 yards 3/8″ diameter. Don't use clothesline with a wire core, which could rust.

Warping Method: Continuous. Stretch the cord as tight around the pegs as possible without bending them. Sew the ends of the cord to the second warps, using a fine needle and thimble. Piercing this warp is difficult, but sewing is better than taping warp ends to adjacent warps.

Warps Per Inch: 2

Number of Warps: 45 (odd number required)

Weft: The background is cream-colored knit fabric with a fine looped pile on one surface, 46 yards 2-1/4″ wide. An old chenille bedspread might be another option. Accent wefts are brown and light orange terrycloth from towels, 5 yards of brown and 7 yards of orange, both 1-1/4″ wide. Remove hems and decorative borders. To stabilize this ravel-prone fabric, machine-sew close to the cutting lines before making strips; I fluffed the strips for a few minutes in my dryer to remove some lint.

Weft Rows Per Inch: 2

Number of Weft Rows: 27 (odd number required)

Instructions

Leave weft segments loose and fluffy. Work from both ends toward the center.

Twine four rows of cream, one row of brown, and one more row of cream.

Cut the cream weft that's on top of the selvedge warp and sew on the orange weft. Twine three rows, alternating cream and orange and keeping the cream weft on top of the selvedge at each edge turn to align the colors vertically.

The center of the mat is solid cream (mine took nine rows). End the rug somewhere in the center section.

Fabric samples; warp on the left.

REMEMBERING LILLIE

Welcome Mat:
24″ x 16″

Estimated Time:
9 hours

Techniques:
Countered twining,
dovetailed tapestry

Dedicated to the memory of Lillie Sherwood, this cheery mat is inspired by one of her finest rugs and uses her distinctive tapestry join. The warp and border are her favorite color — purple — framing a hit-and-miss center in bright fabrics. Lillie would have loved the rich velour, recycled from an old bathrobe, which gives this small rug a luxurious look and feel. One floor-length robe yielded enough for both the warp and border weft.

Frame: Pegged frame, 26″ wide x 18″ long, same as for *Barefoot Delight*

Warp: Purple velour knit, 23 yards long 1-3/4″ wide

Warping Method: Continuous

Warps per Inch: 2

Number of Warps: 45 (odd number required)

Weft: The borders are purple velour knit, same as the warp, 26 yards 1-3/4″ wide. I used 13 solid-colored knits for the hit-and-miss center, 1-3/4″ to 2″ wide, 12″ to 18″ long (37 yards total).

Weft Rows Per Inch: 2-1/2

Number of Weft Rows: 39 (odd number required)

Instructions

Twine six rows of solid purple. Begin the tapestry blocks on the seventh row. The shared warps are the sixth warps in from each side. The side borders form two narrow blocks; the center is one large tapestry block.

For the hit-and-miss center, sew on short sections of weft as you go, or machine-sew different-colored wefts into strips one to two yards long. Because colors change frequently, the same color will not always perform the tapestry join. The strand *on top of* the warp *next* to the shared warp wraps *under* and around the shared warp, then *under* the adjacent warp on the next row. Purple wefts alternate with wefts of other colors around the shared warps.

Work from both ends, finishing this rug on the sixth row of solid purple from the bottom.

Join and hide two purple wefts from one side, two strands from the center, and four strands of purple from the bottom border.

Fabric samples; warp (also used for weft) at upper left.

JUST JEANS

Rectangular Rug:
24" x 36"

Estimated Time:
16 hours

Techniques:
Countered and same-pitch twining, with edge-turn variations

*M*ade of recycled denim with simple patterning, this "country" rug works up quickly. I used parts of ten pairs of jeans, although with less color variation, five or six pairs might be enough.

Light and dark sides of the same blue denim create subtle color differences for the checkerboard rows at the top and bottom. To show the pattern more distinctly in the same-pitch and center rows, I used dark and light wefts from different jeans.

At the top and bottom, deliberately frayed edges of torn denim are a design element, although the "fringe" may become less evident after the rug is in use. I divided the strips from each pair of jeans into equivalent piles for each end of the rug. I folded the relatively stiff wefts in half to twine and sew on new wefts.

The rug buckles slightly where the pitch changes at the ends of same-pitch sections, which is normal. This should lessen after a rug is in use, but if it is a safety concern, avoid same-pitch patterning. Countered twining on the ends keeps the corners flat.

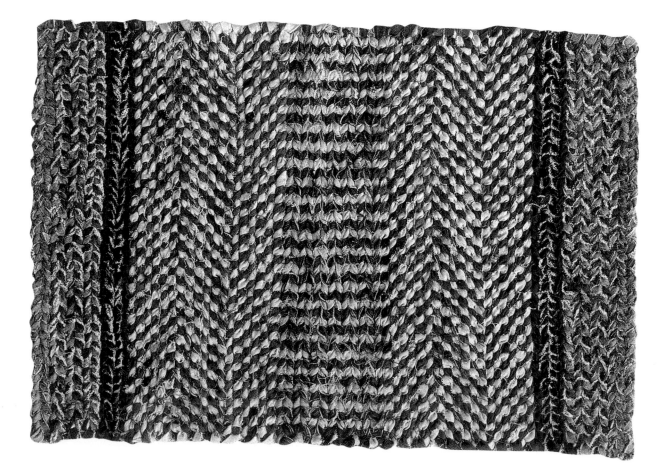

Frame: Frame with suspended wires
Warp: Heavy denim, 1″ wide x 37″ long, sewn into loops 72″ in circumference; total length about 49 yards. Reserve 8 additional yards of this fabric for the first and last weft rows.
Warping Method: Warp loops
Warps Per Inch: 2
Number of Warps: 48 (24 loops). An odd number will also work.
Weft: Heavy denim, 1″ wide, and medium-weight denim, 1-1/4″ wide: dark blue, 37 yards; faded blue (including reverse side of dark blue), 16 yards; light blue, 24 yards; red, 4 yards.
Weft Rows Per Inch: 2
Number of Weft Rows: 37

Fabric samples; warp at left, showing both sides used for weft contrast.

Instructions

In regular countered twining, twine two rows with denim left over from warping (both wefts the same). Work six rows in countered checkerboard twining, using dark and light sides of the same or different jeans. Work one row of red denim, two rows of dark blue, and another row of red.

In same-pitch twining, with dark and light blue wefts, work six rows with left pitch, six with right pitch, and six more with left pitch. With an even number of warps, start the same-pitch rows on one end with the dark color on top, and on the other end with the light color on top. If you use an odd number of warps, start the same-pitch section (row 13) with the same color on top of the selvedge warps.

For the center, switch to countered twining and the edge-turn variation that gives vertical stripes. The first row of the center has the same pitch as the previous row. With an even number of warps, the center area has dark weft on one selvedge and light weft on the other. An odd number of warps will keep the same color on top of both selvedges. Complete as many rows as needed (I used 13) to finish the rug in countered twining in the center section.

TWINED AND INTERTWINED

Rectangular Rug:
25" x 37"

Estimated Time:
36 hours

Technique:
Countered taaniko

A Celtic knot pattern provides the visual pun and name for this rug. Napped fabrics soften its appearance. To avoid the slight streaking evident in my rug, align the nap of the weft in the same direction each time you start a new strip.

The sewn-on velour binding hides the warp ends and frames the pattern, while it helps disguise selvedge irregularities.

Frame: Frame with suspended wires
Warp: Light grey brushed nylon knit, 74 yards 2″ wide
Warping Method: Continuous
Warps Per Inch: 3
Number of Warps: 73. This project requires an odd number of warps if you use the same graph and warp/weft spacing. If you use a different number of warps, make pattern adjustments by adding or subtracting segments in the grey background.
Weft: Light grey suede-like fabric (brushed nylon), 224 yards 2″ wide; dark grey corduroy-textured knit, 52 yards 1-1/2″ wide; red velour 45 yards 1-1/4″ wide. Reserve some velour for the binding, 4 yards 3-1/2″ wide. I used the pattern fabrics as the hidden wefts on the sides, to conserve the background weft. Most of the hidden weft is dark grey, because I had more of it.
Weft Rows Per Inch: 3
Number of Weft Rows: 107 (odd number required)

Fabric samples; warp (also used for background weft) at left.

Instructions

Refer to the graphs on pages 92 and 93. For a rug this same size with the pattern symmetrical and centered, maintain three warps and three weft rows per inch. If by choice or by chance you have a different spacing, you may use the same pattern to twine rugs of other sizes. For example, with 2-1/2 rows per inch in both directions, the same number of warps (73) will make a rug slightly more than 29″ wide, and the warps need to be 43″ long.

For other sizes, determine the warp and weft spacing and divide these numbers into the number of warps and weft rows in the pattern (73 warps and 107 weft rows). Using this pattern at two warps and wefts per inch, the finished rug would be approximately 36-1/2″ wide (73 ÷ 2 = 36-1/2) and the warp would have to be 53-1/2″ long (107 ÷ 2 = 53-1/2).

The pattern consists of squares 1″ wide x 1″ tall, each square requiring three weft segments across and three weft rows.

With two warps and two rows per inch, you can make approximately the same size rug (25″ x 36″) by starting the pattern on the tenth row and making each square ("stair step") in the pattern two warps across and two rows high. However, this will give an even number of rows for the pattern area and the rug (72 total). Therefore, after starting the rug working left to right, you would need to start the other end working *right to left* with a *right* pitch in order to maintain countered twining in the last rows. You would need 50 warps, each 36″ long.

If you are unsure you can maintain a consistent weft-row spacing, twine a few solid-color rows at the top and bottom, then start new wefts for the pattern areas, leaving a little space. Don't trim the original wefts; later you may need to sew more onto them. Mark the halfway point of the selvedge warps. Twine and center the pattern area. Measure frequently to move rows up or down a few at a time, rather than trying to move all the pattern rows at once. Then go back and fill in the top and bottom of the rug, adding onto the starting wefts as needed and maintaining countered twining.

Follow the graph carefully; instructions are for the version on page 93. Use the background weft fabric (light grey) for both wefts for the 13 rows at the top and bottom, in countered taaniko.

If you start at the upper left with a left pitch, the first pattern row will have a right pitch. There are 81 pattern rows; complete the entire pattern area without turning the frame. Sew on red or dark grey wefts as needed; in some rows, rapid color changes require frequent joins. If the rug buckles while you are working the pattern, pull tighter or experiment with narrower pattern wefts until you find a good balance.

Finish the rug in the solid light grey area near the bottom. Hand-sew a binding of red velour on all four sides (optional), turning raw edges under 1/4″ and mitering the corners.

Graph for Twined and Intertwined, two warps and weft rows per inch.

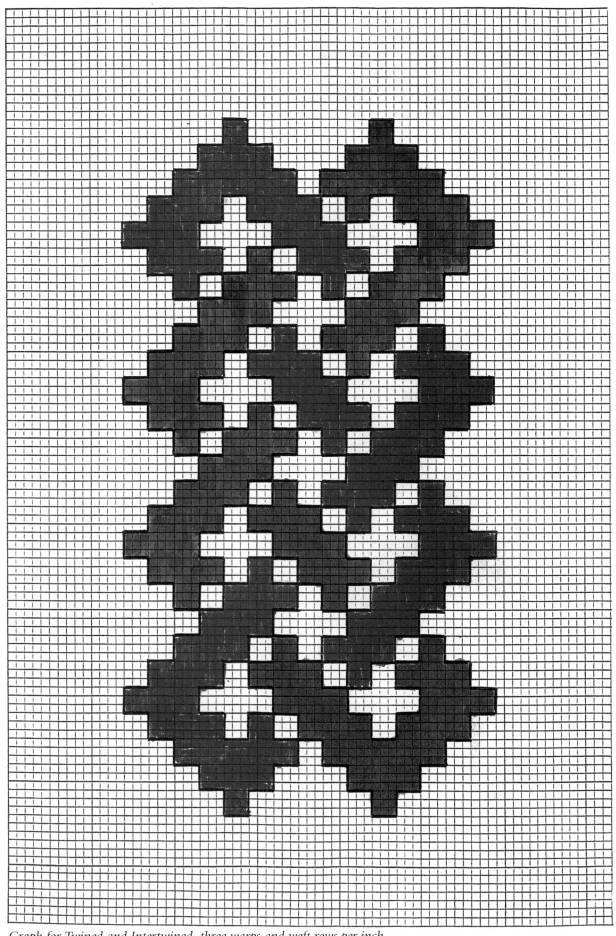

Graph for Twined and Intertwined, three warps and weft rows per inch.

CANYON COUNTRY

Rectangular Rug:
41″ x 27″

Estimated Time:
28 hours

Techniques:
Countered twining ,
false tapestry

*D*ifferent fabric shades and textures give the illusion of light, shadow, and depth to this pictorial rug, which reflects the colors and shapes of the American Southwest. The relatively continuous bands of color make this design appropriate for false tapestry. The rug is reversible, but the front side is more attractive, where weft joins are less apparent.

Frame: Frame with suspended wires, sideways
Warp: Medium blue knit, 1-1/2" wide, and tan herringbone-print knit, 1-1/4" wide, 54 yards total. The warp stretched from its original 24" length during twining, making the finished dimension 27". The pattern allows some leeway to add or subtract rows as needed in the foreground.
Warping Method: Warp loops. Because the top of this rug is a different color than the bottom, I sewed tan and blue warp together to form each loop, using less of the tan fabric since I had more of the blue. Blue warp strips were 33" long and tan strips 18" long; this includes 3" for overlapping strips, since there are two joins for each warp pair. With warp loops, it's easy to position the colors where you want them.
Warps Per Inch: 2
Number of Warps: 80 (40 loops)
Weft: I selected knit and woven fabrics for their colors and cut them to balance: medium blue stretch knit (sky, same as warp) 10 yards 1-1/2" wide; light blue stretch knit (sky) 40 yards 2-1/4" wide; white/blue printed knit (cloud) 12 yards 2" wide; green velour (trees) 32 yards 1-1/2" wide; shiny orange woven fabric (cliffs) 10 yards 3" wide; dark red knit (shadows) 4 yards 2-1/4" wide; medium orange knit (slopes) 25 yards 2-1/4" wide; dark blue cotton nainsook (distant mesa) 8 yards 3" wide; mottled green knit (distant field) 2 yards 1-1/2" wide; solid tan knit (foreground) 40 yards 2" wide; tan herringbone-print knit (dune, same as warp) 34 yards 1-1/4" wide.
Weft Rows Per Inch: 2-1/2
Number of Weft Rows: 68

Instructions

I worked this rug from a sketch rather than a graph, which allowed me to alter patterns and add or subtract rows. The graphed version shows the actual finished weft segments. Feel free to make changes as you work.

Most color changes occur away from the selvedges. A few rows have short color sections, requiring frequent weft changes, but most design areas are continuous for at least several inches. Precise color placement is important when joining wefts.

Follow the graph or sketch (pages 96 and 97), changing wefts as needed. Work most of the rug from the top down, for the best view and control of the developing pattern. Finish this rug within one of the solid tan areas, where you have the most freedom to add or subtract rows without affecting the overall design.

Fabric samples; the two strips at upper left are used for both warp and weft.

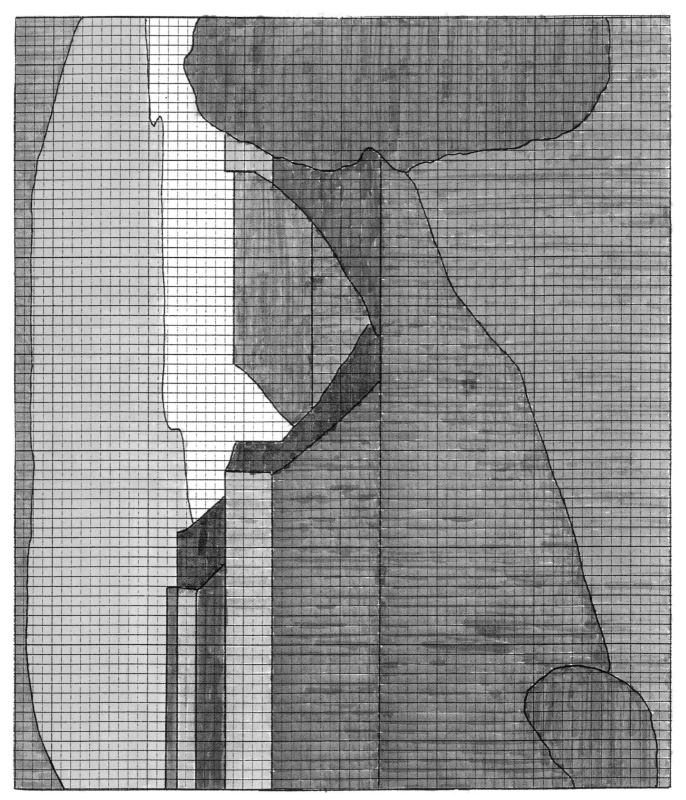

Sketch of Canyon Country.

Graph of Canyon Country.

SPIRIT
OF THE
NORTHWEST

Oval Rug:
27″ x 40″

Estimated Time:
29 hours

Techniques:
Right-pitch twining,
worked clockwise; regular same-pitch twining
in solid and alternating-color rows, taaniko
in pattern areas.

This rug is inspired by Nuu-chah-nulth rugs from Vancouver Island, British Columbia. The whales are modified from several Nuu-chah-nulth rugs. The vine-like band near the outer edge appears on several old rugs and baskets; it visually replicates the taaniko twining action used to create it. The asymmetrical waves, whales, and "vine" add a feeling of motion.

Frame: None; hoop or frame optional

Warp: Navy blue knit, 90 yards 1″ wide. Start with 35″ strips (each serves as two warps) and fold them in half to add warp pairs at the sides. As the rug increases in size, 24″ lengths are adequate.

Warping Method: 29 parallel strips on a flat surface; radial warps added at sides as needed.

Warps Per Inch: 2 to 2-1/2 (varies as warps are added)

Number of Warps: 58 to start, 204 total

Weft: Light grey knit, 65 yards 1-1/2″ wide; magenta velour, 15 yards 1-1/4″ wide; medium blue velour, 18 yards 1″ wide; light blue knit, 95 yards 1-1/2″ wide; navy blue knit, same as the warp, 45 yards 1-1/4″wide.

Weft Rows Per Inch: 3

Number of Weft Rows: 82 (continuous spiral)

Fabric samples; warp fabric on left was also cut a little wider for weft (right).

Instructions

To keep the rug flat, pack wefts without pulling the warps, and add warps as needed. Lay 29 strips side by side, or fringe a solid piece of fabric by cutting strips slightly more than halfway (uncut section away from you) and then cutting the other half after twining the first four rows. Mark all four ends of the side warps with safety pins, using two pins on the upper left (first) warp. As you add warps, keep them outside these original warps, and keep this first set of warps parallel and at the same spacing.

Refer to the graphs on pages 100 and 101. Using two grey wefts, start at the left and work four rows back and forth in right-pitch twining, as if starting a rectangular rug. It may help to tape down the warps temporarily. The curled corners will flatten out after you complete several rows of spiral twining. Even up the warps so the same amount extends to the top and bottom. Add two pairs of warps on each side.

Continue twining clockwise in spiral fashion, adding new warps on the sides as needed to keep the rug flat. Starting on the first warp, twine one round of magenta. Twine one round of grey, then add a pair of warps on each side and twine a second round of grey. Add two pairs of warps on each side and twine one round of medium blue. Add a *single* warp on the right side, and don't add any more warps for the next

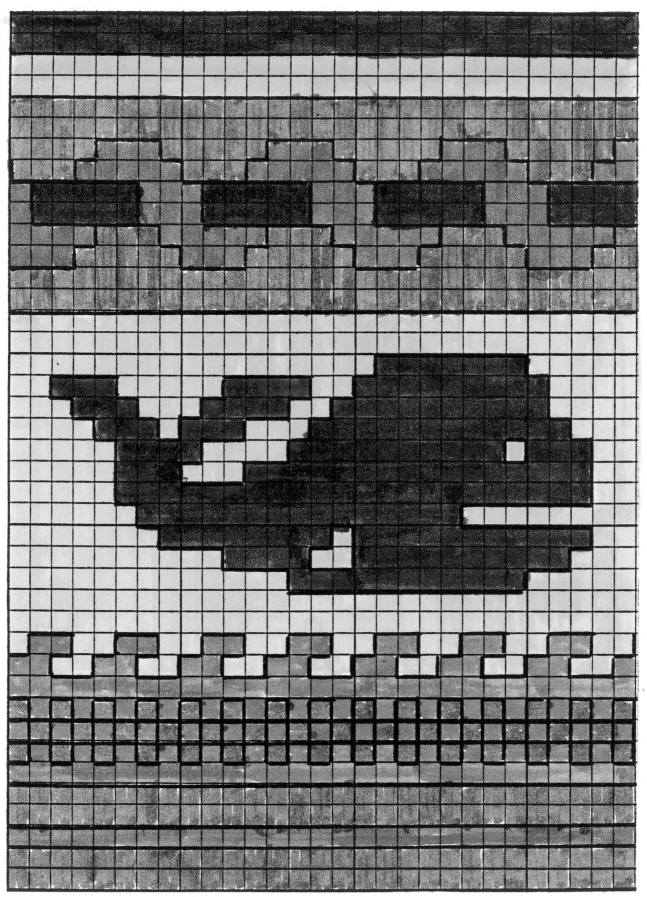

Graph for Spirit of the Northwest, showing the parallel warps at the top half of the rug.

three rounds. Keep one blue weft and start a grey weft on top of the first warp. Work three rounds with alternating blue and grey wefts.

Work one round in medium blue, adding five pairs of warps on each side and a *single* warp on the left side. To make the "waves," work the next two rounds in taaniko with dark and medium blue wefts, starting with medium on top of the first warp and alternating two medium, two light. At the end of the first round, twine *three* light segments in a row (ending on top of warp #1) and continue with two medium, two light, the rest of the way around. Work two rows in light blue with regular twining.

The next row starts the whales; add four pairs of warps on each side. Use two light blue wefts and regular twining except in the pattern areas, where you use taaniko with navy and light blue wefts. Follow the graph from the bottom up, starting with navy on top of the 14th warp. The first whale row takes 11 navy, 47 light, 11 navy, and 47 light segments to complete the round.

On the third whale row, add three pairs of warps on each side. On the 7th round, add four pairs each side, and on the last round, add three pairs on each side. Twine two rounds of light blue in regular twining.

Twine two rounds of grey (regular twining). After the first round, count warps. The "vine" has a pattern repeat of eight segments and requires a multiple of eight warps.

Even if you already have a multiple of eight, you must add enough warps to complete the next six rounds without adding any more. On the second grey round, I added seven pairs of warps on each side (184 total).

Start the pattern band with one magenta and one grey weft, following the graph from the bottom up and beginning with magenta on the first warp. Use taaniko. The sequence for the first round is three magenta followed by five grey, repeated. At the end of this round, twine *four* grey and one magenta; the end of the next round has two grey and two magenta. The third and fourth rounds use magenta and navy, and the final two rounds use grey and magenta.

Above the "vine," in regular twining, work two grey rounds. Add five pairs of warps on each side at the start of the second grey round. Complete the rug with two rounds of light blue and two rounds of navy. Working counterclockwise, pull each warp into the rug on the back side, parallel to an adjacent warp, alternating through four and five rows; trim the excess.

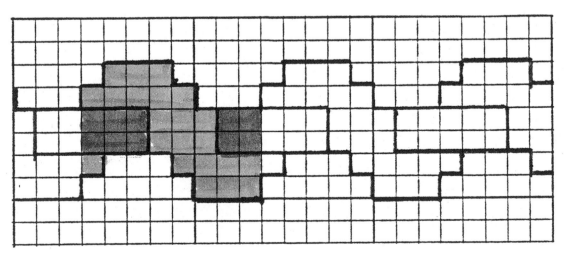

Graph for the "vine" pattern; the colored section is one pattern repeat.

North Star

Runner:
20-1/2″ x 48-1/2″

Estimated Time:
25 hours

Technique:
Regular countered
twining
and taaniko

The banded patterns in this runner, borrowed from Salish rugs, give you leeway to add or subtract rows as you work, so you can make adjustments if you aren't able to maintain the same weft spacing. Tapesty, false tapestry, and taaniko are options for the angular designs; I worked them in taaniko, which is faster, easier, and gives smoother results.

A Salish loom is ideal for a long rug like this. Since the warp is supported at the halfway point, it's easier to maintain straight selvedges than on a larger frame, and it's easy to keep the working area at a comfortable position.

Frame: Salish loom with dowels positioned 2′ apart

Warp: Dark red knit, 70 yards 1-1/4″ wide

Warping Method: Reverse warping with a continuous strand and one wire

Warps Per Inch: 2-1/2

Number of Warps: 51

Weft: Dark red knit (same as warp), 170 yards 1-1/4″ wide; tan checked heavy knit, 71 yards 1″ wide; rust lightweight knit, 40 yards 1-1/2″ wide.

Weft Rows Per Inch: 2-1/2 to 3

Number of Weft Rows: 131

Fabric samples; warp (also used for background weft) at left.

Instructions

Refer to the graph on page 104. Start the warp at the upper left, looping around the wire and pinning temporarily. Reverse direction each time you bring the warp around the wire. Be careful not to pass the warp through the center of the frame except to wrap it around the wire. End at the upper right, coming down from the top roller, and pin the warp temporarily. You need 51 warps (count below or above the wire). Sew the start of the warp to the adjacent warp below the wire. Check to make sure no warps cross through the center of the frame; you must be able to rotate the entire warp and wire around the dowels. Tension should be even but not extremely tight; you must be able to fit two fingers between the warp and the top of the top dowel.

Starting 1″ to 2″ below the wire, twine one row of red in regular twining. Don't use any warps from the back layer. If you add or subtract warps, maintain an odd number and adjust the pattern to keep it symmetrical. Sew the end of the warp to its adjacent warp above the wire and move the first row up by pulling *pairs* of warps. Move the wire to the top of the top roller and mark the halfway point on the warps at the base of the bottom roller.

Graph for North Star, including the entire center section.

Use taaniko for rows two through eight, with tan and red wefts, following the graph.

Use regular twining and red wefts for the next six rows (you can add or subtract rows in this area). Start the star 5-1/2" down from the top.

I used taaniko for the entire rows that make up the side points of the stars and taaniko for the top and bottom points only, with regular twining alongside. My rug has seven rows of solid red, in regular twining, below the star; you can add or subtract rows in this area.

I started the center band about 3-1/4" above the halfway mark, using taaniko for the entire band, with tan and rust wefts. You can expand or contract this area too, depending on your weft rows per inch. Changing the number of rows alters the pattern; with fewer rows, the upper and lower triangles may meet or turn into hourglass shapes. With more rows, they may be farther apart, with the central diamond wider at the center. The center row of the central diamond should just cover the halfway point of the warp. Complete the center band.

Start at the other end of the rug, working from the wire downward and following the same pattern as the first half. Be sure you twine the warps in the proper order. End somewhere in the red section below the star. Poke ends to the back side and remove the wire before hiding the weft ends.

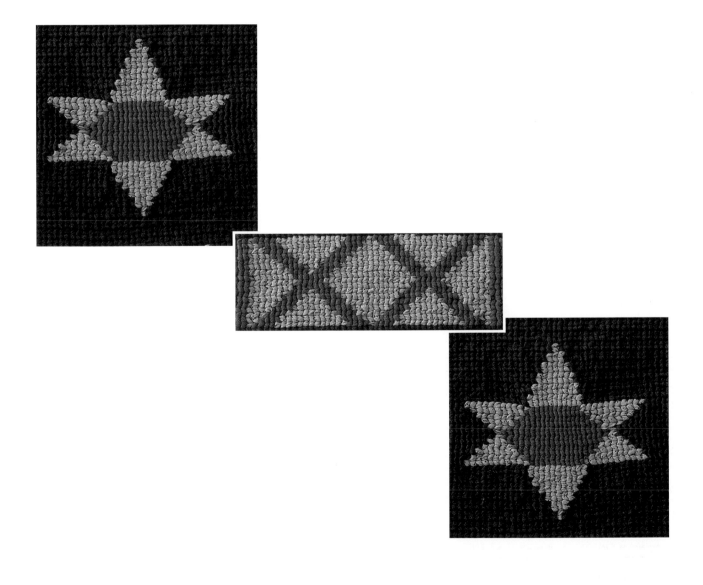

CELEBRATION

Rectangular Rug:
30" x 48"

Estimated Time:
40 hours

Technique:
Countered taaniko twining

*W*hile rummaging through a thrift store, I found an assortment of brightly patterned knit fabrics, already cut into strips just the right width for a twined rug. I purchased additional cotton fabric for the blue starburst. The brilliant colors of the weft fabrics inspired this display of fireworks against a night sky.

Taaniko is the only practical method for twining an asymmetrical, constantly changing pattern like this, where much of the pattern consists of single colored weft segments surrounded by background. I graphed the design first, using photos of fireworks as inspiration, and made minor adjustments as I worked to improve curves and lengthen some pattern lines. Original sampling suggested I'd end up with about 2-1/2 weft rows per inch, and the actual rug has closer to three rows per inch. By marking the center of my graph and the warp, I could tell how close I was coming to my original design, and I was able to add pattern rows to keep the same general dimensions. A freeform design like this allows leeway for changes as you work. The graph on page 108 is the design in its final form, figured for three rows per inch.

The pink, orange, and purple fabrics had more stretch than I normally use, but I couldn't resist the wild fabrics! To compensate, I deliberately twined them more loosely than normal, taking care not to stretch them too much.

Frame: Frame with suspended wires

Warp: Black knit fabric, 1″ wide, 97″ strips, sewn into loops 8′ in circumference, 87 yards total. Each strand is twice the desired length of the rug plus the width of the warp strip.

Warping Method: Warp loops. With the frame upright, distribute loops evenly across the top wire, with supports at regular intervals. Then slip the lower wire into the bottom of the warp loops, with supports to keep the wire from bending.

Warps Per Inch: 2

Number of Warps: 64 (32 loops)

Weft: The background and the hidden weft adjacent to pattern areas is a brushed black knit fabric, 415 yards 1″ wide. Three of the weft fabrics are stretch knits in wild prints, 1-3/4″ wide: pink, 17 yards; orange, 11 yards; and purple, 19 yards. Since I couldn't find a blue knit to match, I used a cotton batiste print, 13 yards 2″ wide.

Weft Rows Per Inch: 3

Number of Weft Rows: 137

Fabric samples; warp (also used for background weft) at left.

Instructions

Refer to the graph on page 108. Twine the entire rug in taaniko, even when using two wefts of the same color. At the ends and alongside pattern areas, use black for the hidden weft. Twine one or two rows of solid black on one end and then rotate the frame and work from the top down. Following the graph, twine six rows of solid black; the first pattern row is the seventh row, and it has only a few colored segments near the right side. Cut the hidden black weft and fasten on a pink strand a few segments before you reach the pattern area. If you've started the rug with a left pitch at the upper left corner, you will work the seventh row left to right also, with 46 black segments, then three pink, two black, two pink, and 11 black to finish that row. (It's easier to count from the right side, starting the pattern on the 18th warp from the right; mark that warp temporarily with a safety pin.)

Continue twining, following the graph and keeping track of where you are by referring to the previous row. Maintain three weft rows per inch to avoid pattern adjustments. If you have less than three rows per inch, subtract a few rows from the graph at the lower end of each starburst. If you have more than three weft rows per inch, add more rows of pattern. Pay attention to the center of the graph and measure the rug as you twine, so you can position the motifs in about the same places they appear on the graph.

Work the entire pattern area from the top down. Rotate the frame to finish in a black row near the end of the rug.

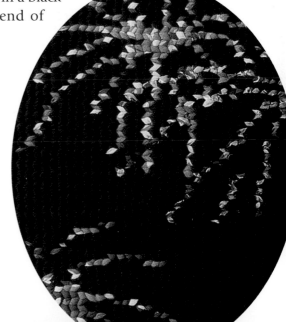

*Graph for
Celebration.*

These sunny colors alone will warm your floor! Not all rugs have to be carefully planned ahead of time. This one evolved as it grew, starting with a bright assortment of fabrics in shades of orange and blue. All of the fabrics in this rug are woven, deliberately cut narrower than usual to reduce bulk and to better approximate the warp and weft spacing in rugs from the Pacific Northwest.

I prefer to cut warps full length from the start, but you can start with shorter warps and sew on additional lengths as needed. This way you can also make a rug larger than you originally intended. Twine a large circular rug on a counter or table, rotating it as you work. Keep the rug as flat as possible. Add warps regularly, evenly spaced. Most of the time the warps are shorter than the wefts, and it's easier to move a warp into the next weft twist than to manipulate long wefts around the warps.

Keep weft rows snug, but to minimize distortion, don't pull too much on the warps. Add warps on solid-colored rows where they will not disrupt a pattern.

Circular Rug: 36″ in diameter

Estimated Time: 36 hours

Technique: Regular right-pitch twining, worked clockwise. You may work counterclockwise with a left pitch.

Frame: None; hoop optional

Warp: Orange-red cotton nainsook, 120 yards 1″ wide. Cut strips at least 8″ longer than the finished diameter of the rug (minimum of 44″ to start); each strip serves as two warps. As the diameter of the rug increases, new warps can be shorter but they must extend at least as far as the original warps. For most of this rug, I used an even number of warps. Where I wanted a spiraling pattern, I added a single warp (odd total number).

Warping Method: Radial

Warps Per Inch: Variable, 2-3 per inch. When you add warps, pull weft segments tight and gradually increase their size until you add more warps.

Number of Warps: 8 to start (4 strips), 242 total

Weft: Woven fabrics, in order of use: red-orange cotton nainsook (same as warp), 85 yards 1″ wide; medium-orange polyester gabardine, 23 yards 1″ wide; gold cotton pongee, 51 yards 1″ wide; mustard heavy cotton, 12 yards 1″ wide; large orange/blue plaid cotton broadcloth, 20 yards 2″ wide; dark blue floral-print cotton batiste, 23 yards 2″ wide; light orange cotton broadcloth, 25 yards 2″ wide; orange/blue plaid cotton/polyester shirting, 9 yards 2″ wide; turquoise heavy cotton, 12 yards 1″ wide.

Weft Rows Per Inch: 2-1/2 to 3

Number of Weft Rows: 63, or until you reach the desired diameter

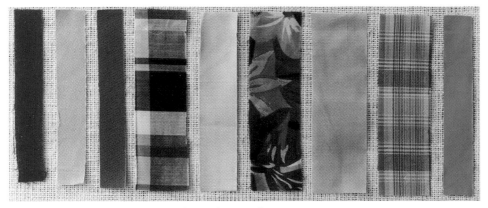

Fabric samples; warp (also used for weft) on left.

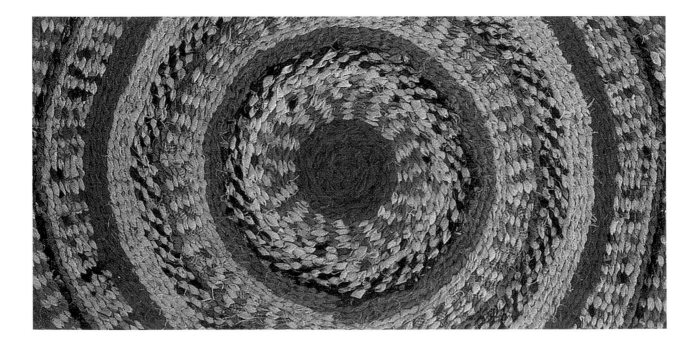

Instructions

Cross four warp strips at their centers, radiating outward at even intervals to create eight spokes. Tack them together at the center to prevent shifting (optional). Choose one warp as the first warp, and mark its end with a safety pin. Leave this pin in until the rug is done, and make all color changes on the first warp.

Use the orange-red fabric (same as warp) for both wefts for the first 11 rows (or until the diameter is 5"). Because it's easy to confuse the warps and wefts at this stage, you can mark the wefts temporarily with pins. Starting around the first warp, twine over and under two warps at a time for the first row only. Continue in a spiral, crossing wefts between each pair of warps and enclosing single warps for the rest of the rug. At a diameter of 4-1/2", add eight pairs of warps evenly distributed (32 total).

At 5" diameter, switch to one gold and medium orange wefts. At 7" diameter, add eight pairs of warps (after each fourth existing warp, 48 total). Continue twining until the diameter is 8-1/2", then twine two rows with mustard and large plaid. At a diameter of 9", add eight pairs of warps (64 total) and twine one row with two mustard-colored wefts.

For the next row, use orange and blue wefts and add a *single* warp (65 total). Twine four rows or 1-1/4". The pattern spirals instead of radiating, because of the odd number of warps. Twine one row with two blue wefts, adding 23 warps (11-1/2 pairs, 88 total).

Work three rows of medium orange and two rows of gold. At a diameter of 15-1/2", add 16 warps (eight pairs, 104 total), and twine four rows (1-1/4") with peach and small plaid wefts. At a diameter of 17-1/2", add 26 warps (13 pairs, 130 total) and twine one row of solid turquoise.

To create the spiraling pattern again, add a single warp and twine four rows (1-1/4") with blue and light orange wefts. At a diameter of 21", add 25 warps (12-1/2 pairs, 156 total); you can cut these warp strips half the original length, as long as each new warp is at least as long as the originals. Twine four rows (1-1/4") of gold and four rows (1-1/4") of orange-red. At 24-1/2" diameter, add a pair of warps after every 12th existing warp (26 warps, 182 total).

With light orange and large plaid wefts, twine five rows or 1-3/4". At 27-1/2" diameter, add 20 warps (ten pairs, 202 total) and twine one row of solid orange and one of solid turquoise. Work one row of blue, then three rows (1") of medium orange and gold. At 32" diameter, add 40 warps (20 pairs, 242 total) and finish twining with orange-red wefts, until the diameter is 36".

On the back side, use a crochet hook to hide each warp alongside an adjacent warp. Pull some warps through three rows of weft and alternate warps through four rows to reduce bulk. Don't pull too hard or you might distort the rug. Trim the excess. Minor bulges tend to disappear with use, as long as you've added enough warps as you worked, and you haven't pulled them too tightly.

DESIGNING YOUR OWN RUGS

Design striped and hit-and-miss rugs as you twine; the number of warps or rows makes little difference, so long as you maintain countered twining. Detailed patterning requires some planning. Try to incorporate some leeway into a design, so you're not restricted to a specific warp and weft spacing, number of warps, or length. Most of the samplers and projects in this book provide places to adjust a pattern.

If a pattern dictates a specific number of rows, warps, or size, use the tables on pages 36 and 38 to help you plan. Unless you work a rug only in one direction, a rug in countered twining with an even number of rows requires starting the ends from opposite sides, with opposite pitch. The instructions for *Twined and Intertwined* on page 91 suggest some ways you can adjust a pattern.

Since countered twining disrupts the line of some patterns, using at least two segments and rows in each pattern block will make a geometric design smoother.

A stair-stepped design on graph paper will look jagged or smooth in a same-pitch rug, depending on the pitch.

A twined design will resemble its graphed version if you have the same number of warps per inch as weft rows; otherwise, the pattern will be elongated or compressed in a rug. Careful sampling and planning will help you achieve the results you want.

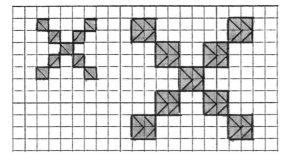

These patterns are similar, but the one with two warps and rows per block will look smoother because of the changing pitch. Pitch direction is indicated by the diagonal lines.

This detail of an old Salish rug shows the effect of pitch on a zigzagged design. Because of the left-pitch twining used for the entire rug, the lines that slant toward the left look smoother than those that slant toward the right. Catalogue #6195, Royal British Columbia Museum. Courtesy Linda Heinrich.

Chapter 5

A Celebration of Rug Twiners

The story of twined rag rugs is really the story of the people who have made them. Men as well as women enjoy rug twining; it's easy enough for small children to learn, and it's therapeutic for the elderly. Rug twiners have diverse backgrounds, as different as their rugs, yet many share common characteristics. Many have northern European ancestry, although few claim that their twining knowledge came directly from Europe. Shared ethnic heritage may be largely coincidental, yet it may have influenced a common work ethic passed down through generations — the desire to make useful things out of "waste" materials.

Most rug twiners have been practical people. They've made rugs because they needed floor coverings. Early in the history of twined rugs, commercial carpeting was scarce and expensive, so many people who couldn't afford rugs (or didn't want to buy them) learned to make their

My grandfather in Denver, Joseph Gütlein, made twined rugs; he was German and had lived in Russia, and he came to Colorado in 1951. He had to settle for the scraps left over after my grandmother picked out the better ones for quilting.

Jean Green
Montrose, Colorado

In the United States, rag twining is especially common in areas settled by Baltic immigrants, so one source may have been northern Europe, birthplace of other rag rug traditions. Lillie Sherwood said her stepfather learned the technique in Denmark before coming to the United States at the age of 12, probably before 1900. She told me, "Everyone in Denmark weaves on frames," and said twined rag rugs were also used as bedcovers, a Scandinavian tradition for other rag rugs. Danish textile historians I have contacted are not familiar with twined rugs from Europe.

A book on Slovakian textiles illustrates a horizontal frame clearly used for twining, although I don't know if the wefts were yarn or fabric. Swiss weaver Silvia Falett first learned of twined rag rugs in a German-language magazine during the 1970s. The article described the work of elderly European twiners and suggested that theirs was a dying art. Silvia also knows of a woman who remembers twined rag rugs from the 1930s in Udine, Italy, on the border of the former Yugoslavia.

If rag twining did originate in Europe, it must have been before 1900 and largely died out there many years ago. Rag twining may have been a home craft outside the regular weaving traditions, which could explain why historians concentrating on loom weaving are not familiar with it.

own. Twining provided durable, practical insulation at almost no cost except for the time involved. It made good use of worn fabrics, appealing to those who couldn't bear to discard anything of potential value.

Most rug twiners learned one method and used it in all their rugs, with little variation except in fabric and color. However, some rugmakers have been especially innovative and creative, experimenting with pattern variations and modifying equipment and warping methods. A few people have actually

Tapestry-twined rug by Langdon Kumler, Indianapolis, Indiana, 1994. Courtesy Langdon Kumler.

I believe in using what materials are available, recycling old materials [rather] than using new ones. There is so much waste in this country; I firmly believe in recycling anything we can use.

Wilma Nelsen, Custer, Michigan

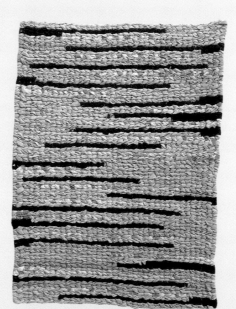
Rug by Wilma Nelsen. Collection of Bobbie Irwin.

Tapestry-twined rugs by Wilma Nelsen, 1998, with her adjustable frame. Courtesy Wilma Nelsen.

I attend many local auctions and am intrigued with the handwork of women, especially things from the 1920s and Depression times. The twined rugs are so typical of women's (and men's) need to make useful and pretty articles from castaways. I was delighted to find a twined rug frame with about 6" of work still intact at an auction.

Caryl Beck
Goose Lake, Iowa

invented twined rag rugs on their own, without having seen them elsewhere. Many twiners independently devised similar equipment and methods.

Despite being practical people, even rug twiners who knew only one method tended to appreciate beauty in everyday objects. A symmetrically patterned rug, with balanced stripes and pleasing color combinations, seems to say, "As long as my maker was going to spend all this time creating me, she decided to take a little extra time to make me pretty".

Even most hit-and-miss rugs were planned to some extent; in some, deliberate border stripes complement the random-colored centers.

Typically, rug twiners like to keep their hands busy, and most enjoy other types of handwork as well. A number of twiners also make other types of rag rugs and enjoy quilting, knitting, crocheting, or weaving.

Some rugmakers display their creations proudly at state and county fairs. Others deny their talents and are astonished when people find their rugs praiseworthy ("It's just rags," they may say). In general, rag twiners derive great satisfaction from making things "from scratch" and find twining a rhythmic, soothing activity. Many of them delight in sharing their skills and knowledge with others. Overwhelmingly, those who make twined rag rugs are enthusiastic about the method and the product.

Few people have made twined rag rugs to sell, probably because of the time it takes to make them and the relatively low prices the public has been willing to pay. Those who have sold their rugs have received very little for their efforts, even when their use of wide weft strips made rapid production feasible.

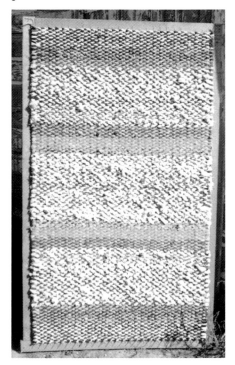

Four-Year Rug by Marty Olsen, Newell, Iowa. Courtesy Marty Olsen.

*W*hen most fabric was handwoven from handspun yarn, people had relatively few clothes, so they didn't have many rags. Rag rugs were uncommon until inexpensive factory-made fabrics became available. About 1850, there was a proliferation of rag rugs of all types; twined rugs apparently date from that period.

The popularity of rag twining has coincided with periods of economic hardship. Use it up, wear it out; make do, or do without. This was the motto of the Great Depression of the 1930s, when twined rag rugs were especially common (although a few people were so poor they had no rags for rugs or quilts). As the economy improved, fewer people twined rugs. A few books and articles during the 1940s and 1950s mentioned the method and may have sparked periodic revivals.

I believe the twiners of the 1930s taught their children, who within a few years could afford to buy inexpensive scatter rugs. Why bother to spend 20 or 30 hours making your own when you could purchase a rug for a few dollars? In addition, the advent of wall-to-wall carpeting at affordable prices soon made scatter rugs less necessary.

For some children of the 1930s, twining was a chore, not a pleasure. In one household, every child twined a row or two before supper every night. Also, the things you see around you every day seem ordinary, and so you may not appreciate their value. While your neighbor's crafts attract your attention, your mother's handwork doesn't seem special. If you grew up with twined rugs in your house, you may have taken them for granted.

A twined rag rug might have been a reminder of hard times. I've heard of a Finnish woman in Montana who twined rugs, but who would not let anybody watch her, perhaps because she was ashamed that she had to make her own. Similarly, I've heard of older women who didn't want others to know they quilted, because they considered it a sign of poverty.

Leslee Barna, Torrey, Utah, is one of several rugmakers who regularly demonstrate twining at the Gifford Historic House, Capitol Reef National Park. Courtesy Leslee Barna.

Josie Pischel, Niobrara, Nebraska (1899-1988), in 1987, with her twining frame and rugs. She also made dozens of braided rugs. Courtesy Pat Fritsche, West St. Paul, Minnesota.

Rug by Clara Rasmussen. Courtesy Ann Haushild, St. Paul, Minnesota.

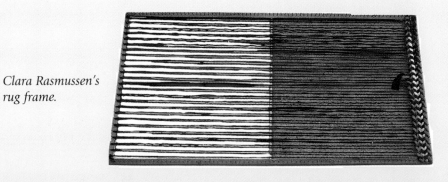

Clara Rasmussen's rug frame.

I have two rugs made by my grandmother, Clara Rasmussen, who lived in Wisconsin. I also have her frame which she warped and did three rows on — so someone could see how she did it, my aunt says. She had crocheted many things and braided rugs for many years and didn't start twined rugs until she was in her mid-'70s. Grandma must have seen a new idea among her rug-braiding friends or in a publication or Home Bureau group. Someone recalls that she found the frame a little cumbersome at her age and didn't do too many rugs as a result.

She always had some project going. While at a home for "old ladies," she got others involved in crafts to help her meet her orders.

Ann Haushild
St. Paul, Minnesota

Today's younger rug twiners tend to be people who value tradition. They treasure the meticulous handwork handed down from their parents and grandparents, and they find satisfaction in reviving old techniques. Twining gives an appreciation of the time and effort that went into making simple household necessities years ago. It is humbling to realize how much our ancestors accomplished without the modern conveniences we enjoy — and it makes us think twice before complaining that we have "no time."

Many of the people who made these rugs died long before I learned about rag twining, and their knowledge and skills died with them. However, thanks to their durability, some old rugs have survived to give clues to the makers' habits and desires. An old rug may hint at the equipment and methods used and may suggest a source for the twiner's knowledge, yet it only tells part of the story. Only by listening to rug twiners and their families and friends can you can get a full sense of the makers' pride in their accomplishments, their enthusiasm for the technique, and the special significance of the fabrics they used.

I have been fortunate to meet and correspond with dozens of rugmakers and their relatives, many of whom were already in their 80s and 90s by the time I contacted them. Here are some of their stories. (With few exceptions, their use

Twenty years ago my great-grandmother lived with us; I was only 13. She made rag rugs, and I loved helping her with them. She would just give them away. I've wanted one of Grandma's rag rugs so badly, but I haven't been able to locate any. So from what I remembered, I made my own wooden frame. I couldn't remember what she warped it with, so I used strips of Levis sewn together.

After spending five hours a day weaving, I finished my rug. It turned out beautifully. I did it all in shades of blue prints mixed together. I did it for my front door mat inside the house, but I'll just die if someone wipes greasy or muddy feet on it!

I'm a person with lots of energy and have to be doing something with my hands all the time. Can't wait to start another rug!

Tonya Post, St. George, Utah

Tonya Post and her first rug. Courtesy Tonya Post.

here of the terms "twined" and "twining" are a response to my questions and articles, and not their original names for the technique.)

My mother, Hannah Washburn, made these rugs for many years. She sent them to the Mormon Women's Handcraft Shop in Salt Lake City [where] they could sell as many as she could make. They paid her $5 for the small rugs and $10 for the large ones.

She usually used old Levis cut into strips for the warp. Occasionally she would use binding twine, but it wasn't as strong as the Levi strips. She usually put stripes on each end of the rug, and the centers were plain. I still have about four of her rugs that she gave me; they do not wear out.

I don't know who taught her to make the rugs. Her mother came to America from Denmark, but I don't remember her ever making the rugs. Grandma had a spinning wheel and made her own wool yarn, but I never saw her make rugs.

Beryl Young, Monroe, Utah

Lillie Sherwood

Born in Kansas May 1, 1900, Lillie moved to southern Idaho in 1910, where she learned how to make twined rag rugs from her Danish stepfather, Nels Nelson, about 1913. "We lived in a big tent while our new house was being built," she remembered. "Daddy hung the rug frame at the top of the tent when it wasn't in use."

When she was 14, Lillie bought a homestead near Idaho Falls, Idaho, and worked her way through business school. When she was 16 she eloped, to avoid the traditional prenuptial shivaree; soon afterwards she and her husband, Archie Sherwood, moved to his hometown of Ogden, Utah. Lillie raised her five children in the Ogden area, working to help support her family even before her husband became disabled. After his death in 1956, Lillie ran a dairy in Riverdale, Utah, until age and highway encroachment induced her to move to her son's ranch in Idaho about 1962.

Lillie told of traveling through the Navajo Reserva-

Lillie Sherwood, 1900-1993.

tion in Arizona many years ago, and of stopping to watch a Navajo woman weaving a rug by the side of the road. Although the women didn't speak the same language, their hands did. Eager to share her knowledge, Lillie tore her apron into strips to demonstrate rag twining on the Navajo warp. (Ironically, the Navajo weaver was probably already familiar with twining, which traditionally is used to space the warp at both ends of a Navajo rug.)

Enthusiastic about twined rugs, Lillie especially appreciated their tendency to lie flat. "They were the only rugs my husband would allow in the house after he became ill," she stated, "because he didn't have to worry about tripping over a curled-up edge." Lillie scouted second-hand stores for the

brighter used clothing (to the dismay of the salesclerks). She used the scarce shades sparingly in her older rugs, concentrating them in the lively patterns which were her hallmark. Later, a daughter's fabric business provided colorful scraps.

Several aspects set Lillie Sherwood's rugs apart. The combination of her tight twining, her uncommon frame and warping variations — wrapping the warp around a plain frame or around suspended rods — made Lillie's rugs especially firm and durable. They are also extraordinarily beautiful because of Lillie's unusual patterns. Sometimes she used false tapestry. Frequently she combined true tapestry with twining to create checkerboard blocks in a multitude of carefully balanced colors.

Lillie probably invented the tapestry version herself. "Daddy showed me how to make the rugs, but I worked out the patterns later. After I started my family, it was several years before I started making rugs again, and I had to teach myself all over again." Several

Detail of a false tapestry rug by Lillie Sherwood.

Two of Lillie Sherwood's tapestry rugs.

tapestry joins are possible in twining; Lillie devised (probably through trial and error) the method that best covers the warp.

Lillie Sherwood's daughter, Lola Cunningham, remembers a rug her mother made her with a red diamond in the center. She still owns two tapestry-twined rugs, and recalls, "As long as I can remember, there was a wood frame, a box of rags, and a rug on the frame."

Most Sherwood rugs I have seen are hit-and-miss, striped, or geometric. However, Lillie evidently made more complex patterns, too. She described a rug with a picture of a house, complete with a path to the door and smoke coming out the chimney (I was never sure if she had actually made this rug or just envisioned it, but I never doubted that she could do it). Animal designs also may have been part of her repertoire.

Lillie Sherwood also found other uses for rag twining, such as car upholstery and saddle girths she made for a leather shop. She was adept at adapting the method to the purpose at hand, using whatever materials were available. And she used almost every type of cloth imaginable, from sturdy denim to sheer curtain fabric, often in the same project.

In addition to saddle girths, Lillie also sold at least one rug. She described finishing a particularly beautiful rug, which she decided to keep. It was so wonderful, she hung it on her wall — quite out of character for this practical woman who believed rugs were to walk on. A visitor saw the masterpiece, declared that he had to have it, and asked Lillie to set a price. Since she didn't want to part with it, she told him the rug would cost him $100 — a high price for a rag rug, even today, and this incident may have happened several decades ago. Without hesitation, the man handed her the money and left with the rug. Lillie was very proud of that sale!

For the most part, rag twining was not a money-making activity for Lillie Sherwood. She said she never had many of her rugs around the house; invariably a visitor would praise a rug she'd just finished, so Lillie would give it away. It is typical of her generosity that her last rug, completed with the aid of a granddaughter about 1982, was her donation to the local high school for a fundraising auction. Made of new fabric in the school colors, with the school initials twined into it, this rug occupies a place of honor in the school trophy case.

Lillie was also generous with her knowledge. Over the years, she probably demonstrated the technique to hundreds of people. Lack of energy, rather than the severe arthritis in her hands, made Lillie give up twining; an expert quilter as well, she continued to enjoy some stitchery. About 1990 she moved into a nursing home in Arco, Idaho, where she died June 6, 1993.

I didn't know what they were called when I did one as a summer project when I was a teenager. That must have been in 1938 or '39.

I was brought up during the Depression. What a big influence that has had in the lives of people of our generation. Young people today would not generally think of what they could do with those worn-out clothes, as we did. I have tried, over the years, to instill in our children some of these traits that I grew up with.

Virginia Pratt, Heyburn, Idaho

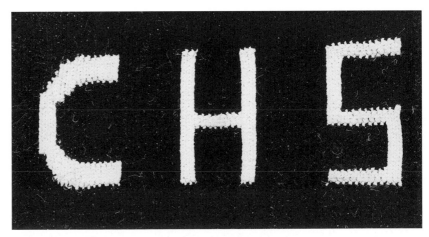

Lillie Sherwood's last rug, with tapestry patterning.

Leona Christensen Lambert

Leona Lambert (1893-1990) as a young woman. Courtesy Nina Whiting, St. George, Utah.

Leona's daughter, Nina Whiting, told me about her mother's rug twining. "My mother was born in 1893 in northern Utah, of Danish and English Mormon pioneers. After her marriage she lived in the Lost River Valley of central Idaho, in a ranching world. She raised seven children and between the never-ending work of ranch life, she was very creative and productive. There wasn't time for frivolity, and her creative talents were directed toward making practical necessities — sewing clothing, making hundreds of quilts, and innumerable rugs.

"She made all kinds of rag rugs, [including] many of the twined rag rugs. I loved to watch her short but strong fingers twisting the strips of fabric about the warp — usually strips of denim. These rugs were thick and very heavy and best washed with a broom and suds, [then] rinsed with a hose. They were wonderfully practical and ideal for absorbing the mud and snow that came through the doorways on ranchers' boots.

"Mom had a carpenter make her twining frame to her specifications -1" x 4" lumber, mitered at the corners, and finishing nails set all around at precise intervals to attach the warp and rags to. How-to books weren't available, and I am amazed at the know-how she had acquired from her forebears in all types of home-making skills. She died in 1990 at the age of 96 years."

Grace Kenfield

Grace Kenfield (1917-1990), Absarokee, Montana. Courtesy Marge Ferrin, Billings, Montana.

One of the few rag twiners to write about the technique was Grace Kenfield, a Montana rancher. Born in Lincoln, Nebraska, in 1917, she moved to Reedpoint, Montana, in 1920. She lived there until her husband's death in 1976 and then moved to nearby Absarokee, where she wrote a humorous newspaper column and book.

Grace, better known by her pen name, GeeKay, didn't use the term "twined" and didn't consider herself a weaver, even though she titled her rag twin-

---

My grandmother used to make them, and she showed me how to weave when I was about 10 or 12 years old. My husband made my rug frame as near as I could remember my grandmother's, but it had been 20 years and was hard to remember.

Zelda Robertson, Lehi, Utah. Courtesy Zelda Robertson.

It takes me about 40 hours to weave a rug — 15 minutes a row and four rows per inch. My first rug has had extremely heavy use for 30 years and is still not worn out, or even badly worn, and has been by the door of a farm house — seven children and now 19 grandchildren.

Zelda Robertson

ing article "Weaving Rugs the Easy Way" [*Profitable Hobbies*, May 1954, p. 24-26 and 48-50; Modern Handicraft (now KC Publishing)]. "I'm no weaver," she wrote. "As far as I'm concerned, 'warp' is what a board does when left out in the rain and 'woof' is what a dog says... [W]here the weaver might say she 'warped' a rug, I say I'm 'stringing' a rug. And instead of weaving it, I'm 'twisting up' another rug."

GeeKay claimed that she started making rugs to warm her feet during cold Montana winters. She was astonished the first time someone asked to buy one, since "It seemed...ridiculous to sell something that had cost nothing but pleasure to make." After selling that rug for the "high price" of $7.50, she eventually (by 1954) raised her price to $10 and sold as many as she cared to make. She also gave many as gifts and carpeted her house with the rest.

"In a pinch, I've made them in a day," she said. Her use of very thick warp (6"-wide strips of old sheets or somewhat narrower strips of denim) and weft (4"-wide strips of cotton or other fabric) made this production speed possible. Although her article discussed how to balance colors for symmetrical borders, hit-and-miss rugs warmed the floor of her Absarokee home. "After the experimental stage, my ultimate aim was to make the rugs enough similar so they'd pass as the carpeting I couldn't afford," she explained.

Evidently rag twining came

down through Grace's family. She began twining when she was in her early 30s and she thought her pegged, adjustable frame might have been her mother's, although she couldn't remember her mother making rugs. "I think my mother picked up this rug weaving from a homemakers' club and had my husband make her a rug frame," she speculated. In a letter to another twiner (Virginia Verdier), she told of a ranch home where a man used the kitchen window frame for twining, and the room got darker as the work progressed!

Grace Kenfield's frame with a rug in progress. Courtesy Marge Ferrin.

Grace Kenfield died in 1990 at the age of 73, and her home was sold at auction. Apparently her dozens of rugs were discarded, although some she made in earlier years may still warm Montana ranch homes. As she said, "They are practically indestructible. I've tried almost every sort of rag rug from...braiding to scraps wrapped on rope; but I have never found a type of rug that passed so many tests as this."

I used to make those rugs years ago in the 1930s. My mother was a rugmaker; it was sort of a profession. She made braided rugs; she also made twined rugs and taught me how.

My husband made me a wooden frame about the size I wanted the rug to be. He drove small nails into the narrower widths on the top and bottom. I tore old overall strips and sewed them together and strung them from top to bottom, forming the base to twine the rags around. Then, using lengths of rags that I had sewn together, I twined them around the overall strips. This made a rather heavy rug.

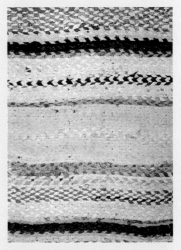

Rug by Wanda Johnson, Ovid, Idaho (1912-1998).

When I was pregnant and couldn't sleep at night, I would get up and work on this rug. By using overalls as a base, it made the rug at no cost except the thread. It was certainly a way of passing the time when I couldn't sleep.

Wanda Johnson

Virginia Verdier

If it can be done with fiber, yarn, or fabric, Virginia Verdier has probably tried it. Her house and outbuildings in Sidney, Ohio, are completely filled with knitting machines, looms, spinning wheels, and other craft equipment and supplies, as well as projects in all stages of completion. In an article about twined rugs she wrote for *Crafts ' n Things* magazine ("Country Carpets," Summer 1981, pp. 16-18), she commented, "You name it, I'll try it. In my opinion, money spent on crafts is that much less you have to pay the doctor."

Introduced to twining by books, Virginia started making rugs in the late 1970s. She attributes some of her inspiration to Osma Gallinger Tod's book, *The Joy of Handweaving* (D. Van Nostrand Co., 1964, "Weaving a Rug on a Frame," pp. 35-39), which describes twining rag rugs on a string warp. However, Virginia's pegged frame, direction of working, fabric warp, countered twining, and accurate terminology are all different from Tod's and reflect her own experimentation, combined with information from other books and rug twiners

Virginia Verdier, right, with her sister-in-law, Henrietta Martin, left.

(including Grace Kenfield).

Virginia's symmetrically striped rugs are unusually thick and heavy, because she cuts her warp fabric at least 3" wide and her weft strips about 4" wide. All her rugs are finished with thick yarn fringe tied onto the warp. Her frame, with adjustable crossbars, does not have any selvedge guides and is similar to Grace Kenfield's.

Virginia has introduced many people to rag twining through classes, demonstrations, and magazine articles. Among those she has taught is her sister-in-law, Henrietta Martin (also of Sidney, Ohio), who has made dozens of twined rugs using bright knit fabrics.

Virginia comments, "People are really interested when they

see how simple [twining] is and what a nice item it produces. I always tell them that before they get the first rug finished, they will have made plans for the next one." Always eager to try something new, she mentioned, "I would like to experiment with making a rug on a round frame — a mix of wagon-wheel, basket-bottom, and twined using the same kind of weft. It would have to be 'round 'n 'round twining instead of the countered twining."

Grace Durfee

Grace Durfee (left) demonstrating twining at an Extension Service conference in 1991, in Logan, Utah.

A resident of Almo, Idaho, Grace Durfee has been making twined rag rugs since about 1933, when a neighbor introduced her to the craft. She has demonstrated twining through Extension Service programs, and her daughters and grandchildren are also expert rug twiners.

Grace's frame is a common pegged version, with nails on four sides. Grace places the edge warps outside the nails to keep selvedges straight. She and her family have called the technique "frame braiding."

Rug by Virginia Verdier, 1992. Courtesy Virginia Verdier.

A daughter, Linda Chappell, of Lyman, Utah, describes her childhood memories. "We had twined rugs in every room in the house. As a child, I helped push the rags through from the back for the last row. Twined rugs are just part of my life. I couldn't work in my kitchen without them." Perhaps more than anyone else in Utah, Linda (a former Extension Home Economist) has kept the tradition alive through Extension Service classes. Her influence is evident in the rugs and frames in her neighbors' homes.

Three generations of this family continue to enjoy rag twining. Linda's sister, Delilah Darrington, has taught twining to church groups. Linda's three daughters also enjoy twining. One daughter's rug won a blue

Linda Chappell with one of her hit-and-miss rugs.

ribbon in a 4-H exhibit at the Utah State Fair in 1991; she and a sister demonstrated twining for a state 4-H contest. One of the girls taught her fourth-grade class how to twine.

*W*ell, they're just rags. I've got two of them made up now, but they're already sold. If you can wait a couple weeks, I ought to have two more made up, and then you can take your pick. It takes me about a week to make one. How many have I made? I stopped counting when I got to 200, and that was several years ago.

I've been making them for about 50 years. I had seen one, but it wasn't very even, and I said, my gosh, I bet I could make better ones. I'm quite a challenger, so I got some boards and nails and put a frame together, and my first one turned out real nice.

My cousin brought her rugs over one day and said, "Millie, I bet you could make rugs like this." I said, "Well, let me show you the ones I've done." And when she saw them, she gathered hers up and said, "Next time, I'm coming to you for lessons."

Mildred Sanders

Mildred Sanders, La Verkin, Utah, in 1999 with one of her recent rugs.

Rug twined by Mildred Sanders at the age of 94. Collection of Bobbie Irwin.

I loved my rug from the first few rows and enjoyed admiring it from across the room. I think the surprising thing about it was what strength was required to tug the twined strips tight and the mess it made with frayed fabrics. Now finished, it resides in our entrance hall, greeting visitors with its mixed-up colors and lovely soft thickness. The rebirth of discards into something practical and beautiful has strong appeal.

Jean Reed

Jean Reed, Campbell, California, with her first twined rag rug. Courtesy Jean Reed.

Nathan Jones

Nathan Jones, Maeser, Utah, 1993, with his first circular twined rug.

Nate Jones is truly an inventor of rag twining, and his prize-winning rugs and other twined work reflect his creative spirit. He's also a skilled woodcarver and basketmaker, and his knowledge of basketry led to his use of rags for twining.

While living in Alaska in the early 1980s, Nate learned how to make intricate twined baskets from grass. Later, without having seen anyone else's twined rugs, he used the same techniques to make circular rag rugs. He twines without a frame, manipulating his rag warps as much as the wefts while he works. Nate crosses a few short warps to start a rug and adds more as needed by looping new warps around the wefts. To change patterns or colors, he may interchange warp and weft. There is nothing static about his methods or his designs, and he makes up his own rules as he goes along.

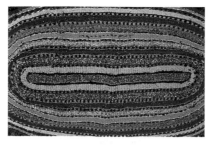

Oval rug by Nathan Jones.

Nate has also applied rag twining to other utilitarian and decorative items, including picture frames and bedspreads. He makes rectangular pieces by fringing a solid piece of fabric to serve as warp, and he has recently started making oval rugs as well. "I just use scissors and my imagination," he explains.

People are always asking me to teach their children to make rugs, and I say no. Wait until they want to do it.

One thing I've learned from making rag rugs is to pick up my feet! Everyone asks me how long it takes to do it, and I say "forever — if you don't get started!

Adeline Starr

Adeline Starr, Huntington, Utah, who specializes in "Shirret" (shirred) rag rugs.

Mary Peters

Mary Peters. Oliver Wells Collection, courtesy Marie Weeden.

Born on New Year's Day, 1901, Mary Peters is known in part for her twined rag rugs. A Salish woman from British Columbia, she is credited in large part with the revival of Salish weaving in the early 1960s.

In 1963, Mary Peters independently reintroduced the old art of twining blankets and rugs, which she remembered from her youth. Mary worked on an upright loom with two crossbars (one adjustable), which she built "from memory of looms previously used by her family for rug-making," according to Oliver N. Wells in "Return of the Salish Loom" (*The Beaver*, Spring 1966, p. 43).

As part of their "civilization" efforts, Canadians had outlawed "potlatch" ceremonies in 1884. A potlatch host would demonstrate his generosity by giving away most of his belongings, especially blankets and other textiles. Missionaries were aghast at this practice, which seemed to encourage poverty, not understanding that potlatch hosts invariably reacquired their wealth at someone else's potlatch. Salish weaving and twining virtually disappeared after potlatches were outlawed, and when Mary Peters resumed rug twining in the 1960s, it is said that she did it in secret because she may have believed the technique itself was illegal.

Members of the Salish Weavers Guild speculate that her first rugs were made with fabric because that was what she had available. I suspect that she had seen twined rag rugs years earlier, since they were still made at least into the 1920s. Perhaps her own family used rags, and she herself might have made twined rag rugs during her younger years.

Soon after Mary Peters resumed twining, her efforts were discovered by Oliver Wells, whose deep interest in Salish traditional crafts led him to encourage their revival. After studying an old Salish rag rug to learn twining, Wells constructed a Salish loom based on early written accounts. During this experimentation, Wells heard of the twining being done by Mary Peters.

Wells described three rugs made by Mary Peters, including two twined with fabric in diamond patterns, using tapestry. One of her rugs is proudly displayed in the Salish Weavers' shop in Sardis, British Columbia. Photographs by Oliver Wells show that Mary Peters twined from the top down, advancing portions of the diamonds before filling in background areas.

As the weaving revival took hold, and at the suggestion of Oliver Wells, Mary Peters used handspun yarn in her later work, primarily blankets and wall hangings. She passed along her skills to a daughter and two granddaughters, as well as to other Salish women. Revered by

Tapestry-twined rug by Mary Peters, 1963.

Mary Peters's rug in progress, 1963; after the photo was taken, she changed the pattern at the right side. Oliver Wells Collection, courtesy Marie Weeden.

Twined rag rug by Mary Peters. Oliver Wells Collection, courtesy Marie Weeden.

the Salish as "The Mother of Modern Weaving," Mary Peters died Jan. 5, 1981, four days after her 80th birthday.

An aunt of my husband's uses a frame made by her father for her mother — way over 50 years old. Her mother also made them on the rim of a buggy wheel. In fact, her mother made mostly the round ones. But the aunt could not perfect her technique for the round ones after her mother died.

Elaine Tweedy's husband, Roger, shows off a rug she made in 1998. Courtesy Elaine Tweedy, Mt. Pleasant, Iowa.

I've been making twined rag rugs for about six months. My first rug was one of just learning how to do it. I now know how not to do it! I will use bobbins to be able to pick up a color to make the design I want — such as in knitting. The next one should be decent. I use a dowel on the sides to keep edges straight. Or I hope they will be on the next rug!

Elaine Tweedy

Fred Gossell

Fred Gossell, St. Cloud, Minnesota. Courtesy J.H. Gossell, Minneapolis.

Born in 1893, Fred Gossell was a barber in St. Cloud, Minnesota. He started twining rugs during the 1930s, after admiring a rug made by an elderly neighbor, Anna Rathburn. His son, J.H. Gossell, remembers, "The family was impressed with the rug because it was so thick and it stayed put on the floor. Dad went over to Rathburns to check out the loom and the weaving process and made a larger frame for himself.

"Those were the days before television," continues Gossell. "The main source of evening recreation was listening to the radio. The loom was always handy, and when my dad wasn't using it, some other family member might weave a few rows (of course with comments from Dad on which colored rags to use to fit in with his scheme). We could listen to the radio or carry on a conversation and still keep the hands moving."

Fred Gossell made smaller frames for smaller projects, such as a piano-bench cover. His primary rug frame, 28" x 48", was a common pegged frame with his own modifications. His son explains, "I remember there was some experimenting before the process went smoothly. A later innovation — after the first or second rug — was the addition of wire rods along the sides, threaded through screw eyes, to keep the middle of the rug from bowing in." To keep the warp from slipping off the nails, Fred wrapped cords in spiral fashion around the nails, warp, and frame at the top and bottom.

Detail of Fred Gossell's frame and selvedge guide.

Fred twined from the bottom up, using a crochet hook to work the last few rows at the top. He would prop the padded frame on a chair to start a rug, then move it to the floor as the work progressed. With multiple strands of cotton string for warp, and cotton rags torn about an inch wide for weft, his rugs have five to six rows of meticulous twining per inch. Most of his rugs are symmetrically striped, with a thick fringe of carpet warp.

"He threaded a heavy string through the loops of the warp as he pulled the rug off the nails. This kept the warp from receding back into the weaving so he could tie on the coordi-

Rug by Fred Gossell.

nating fringe," Fred's son recalls.

During Fred's later years, rug twining served as good therapy for a nervous condition, keeping his fingers busy. His son estimates Fred made dozens of rugs during the 1970s and early '80s, and friends and family still cherish many of them. His last warp was still on the frame when he died at the age of 95. "It's too bad you didn't find out about him a few years earlier," his son mentioned. "Dad would have been in his glory telling you about his hobby."

Rug by Fred Gossell. Collection of Bobbie Irwin.

In 1994 one of Fred Gossell's granddaughters began twining on the warp he had put on the frame shortly before his death, and she soon finished her first rug — with a little help from friends who asked for frames of their own. After winning a sweepstakes award for a rug at her county fair, she taught a couple twining classes. No doubt her grandfather would be pleased.

Silvia Falett

Silvia Falett.

A professional weaver in Ottenbach, Switzerland, Silvia Falett designs and weaves fine fabric for clothing and accessories. A member of the board of the Swiss Handweavers' Association, she exhibits her work extensively and teaches classes in a variety of subjects, including rag twining.

Silvia first read about twined rag rugs during the 1970s when she was learning to weave. Fascinated with the rugs, which had no visible warp, she wondered how to make them. In 1994, Silvia and her husband spent a year in the United States where she saw one of my articles about twined rag rugs. She recognized the technique as the same one that had intrigued her years before, and she arranged to spend a day in my studio studying rag twining.

After returning to Switzerland, Silvia began reintroducing the craft to a new generation of European weavers. She has written articles about twined rag rugs, and our search for their origins, in a Swiss handweavers' magazine and a journal for teachers. She continues to discover information about rag twining traditions in Europe and Québec, Canada.

Rug by Silvia Falett. Courtesy Silvia Falett.

An innovative designer, Silvia inspires her students with her beautiful rugs and other household articles, which she twines in a variety of sizes and patterns. Her determination to revive a disappearing folk art means that twined rag rugs will continue to brighten the floors of homes in her part of the world.

RAG TWINING TODAY

Fortunately, grandchildren and great-grandchildren of the 1930s twiners are rediscovering the values of old handwork, and twining is enjoying a revival. Dencil Gold, from Genola, Utah, remembers his grandmother twining rugs in Idaho, although his mother did not make them.

Dencil Gold works on a horizontal frame.

An old rug by Rosella Jenkins, Tuttle, Idaho, grandmother of Dencil Gold.

After taking a rug-twining class in Alaska about 1984, he started making twined rugs for his children. Tonya Post carries on her great-grandmother's tradition and has passed it on to her daughter. In a few families, twining has continued without a break, and in several cases three generations of a family continue to enjoy rag twining.

Two rugs by Dencil Gold.

As part of a modern revival, numerous rugmakers are learning twining, including many with no family tradition of the technique. You can help assure that this worthwhile craft continues to bring satisfaction and enjoyment to future generations.

Tonya Post's daughter, Tarci Post (age 10), St. George, Utah, demonstrates twining at a folk life festival in 1995. Courtesy Tonya Post.

About the Author

$\mathcal{B}$obbie Irwin has studied twined rag rugs and their history since first seeing them in 1980. A frequent contributor to fiber-art and textile journals, she is recognized as an authority on rag twining and has published articles about the craft in *The Weaver's Journal, Heddle, Piecework,* and *Rug Hooking* magazines. (She insists, though, that the real authorities are the people who have been twining rag rugs for 50 years or more!)

Since 1985, Bobbie has lectured and taught classes about twined rag rugs throughout the United States and Canada. Her research continues, on a worldwide scale, as she works to determine the origins of rag twining and to revive this fascinating craft for the enjoyment of future generations.

Twined Rag Rugs is the first complete book on rag twining and the only resource to include the numerous variations in equipment, pattern, and twining techniques, both traditional and modern.